Walks in the Chiltern Hills

18 circular walks described in detail

with historical places and points of

interest to engage the walker in

moments of rest along the way

By Leslie Ham

Order this book online at www.trafford.com
or email orders@trafford.com

Most Trafford titles are also available at major online book retailers.

Printed in the United States of America.

ISBN: 978-1-4669-1433-9 (sc)
ISBN: 978-1-4669-1435-3 (hc)
ISBN: 978-1-4669-1434-6 (e)

Library of Congress Control Number: 2012902305

Trafford rev. 02/09/2012

 www.trafford.com

North America & international
toll-free: 1 888 232 4444 (USA & Canada)
phone: 250 383 6864 ♦ fax: 812 355 4082

Contents

By the same author

The Orange Way

This is a 350 mile walk in the footsteps of history. It follows the march in 1688 by Prince William of Orange and his army from Brixham in Devon, across the English countryside to London. It links the walker to the unfolding story of the "Glorious Revolution", highlighting which took place on or near the route.

The Nelson Way

This is a 424 mile walk following a route from Burnham Thorpe in Norfolk finishing at HMS Victory in Portsmouth. It links together many locations associated with Horatio Nelson from his birthplace to his flagship. It goes along coastal and riverside paths, though towns and villages, over hills and across valleys but it is never far from an overnight hostelry, railway station or bus route. It links the walker to the unfolding story of England's greatest sailor whilst highlighting the locations associated with Nelson.

The Surrey Hills

19 circular walks and 1 linear walk from 7½ miles upwards are described in detail through the delightful Surrey Hills with local historical commentary to enliven those moments of rest. The walks go through villages, over hills parkland and heathland. The Roof of Surrey walk takes in a loop of the best known hills encompassing all the highlights surrounding the Tillingbourne valley.

www.leshambooks.com

Preface

Walking is a basic movement of mankind. He might have walked from place to place for survival, to follow a food supply, or avoid harsh or changing weather patterns, then later to tend his captive animals and manage his crops. It is only since mankind had conquered his basic requirements and safeguarded his food supply that he chose to walk for reasons not particularly connected with survival. With walking we need only free time to become available to us as a pleasure rather than a necessity as the act of walking costs little. This has led in the past to a perceived division of attitude in the social classes – those who rode and those who walked – the wealthy and the poor.

However, there have been many notable walkers in history, Poets, Intellectuals, Pilgrims, Explorers and Ramblers among them. Probably some of the first walkers to be noticed were the Pilgrims walking great distances for their faith.

Walking is easy providing one is fit and able, as implied by the commonly used phrase "It's a walk in the park". In reasonable health it's just a question of putting one foot in front of the other and repeating it. Walking is the art of the lingering revelation. Something spied in the distance comes to us slowly and quietly. The distant feature is upon us, then offering new horizons to the adventurous. Walking loses its measurable distances in favour of the passage of time.

Walking is one of life's natural ways to maintain the health that each of us was probably and thankfully born with. It needn't be a marathon or a daunting hill climb, a walk can be broken down into easy segments enabling those who thought they couldn't, can. With reasonable health walking is always available to those who have denied it a place in their lives.

Walking for pleasure allows us to create our own plan, when to walk, where to walk, how far to walk, at what speed, where to pause;

> What is this life if full of care
> We have no time to stand and stare

It offers us an opportunity to expand an interest be it in flora and fauna, ornithology, lepidoptera, wildlife, geography, geology, history, architecture, even literature and music; therefore walking provides us with that vehicle. It allows us to observe at a more leisurely pace lending itself to thought and ponder. It is an antidote to modern speed living where time passes by unchecked. It lends itself to personal achievement at one's own will in a governing age.

LH
Weybridge 2012

Acknowledgements

Marlow public library
Henley public library
High Wycombe public library
British Library, London
Additional photography: Maureen Clarkson
Route Checkers: Robert Allen, Sue Emmett, David Emmett,
David Grigg, Gill Heaven, Brian Maunder,
Inge Mikkelsen, Marilyn Payne, Tilly Smith,
Peter Stone
Susan Maguire, Henley and Goring Ramblers for recruiting her
group's volunteer checkers
Proof reading: David and Anne Grigg

Front cover pictures
Cobstone windmill overlooking Turville
Tortoiseshell Butterfly
Chilterns view
Red Kite

Rear cover pictures
St Mary's church, Hambleden
Old school sign, Turville
Village sign, Russell's Water
St Nicholas church, Britwell Salome
Memorial gate, near Henley Park, Oxfordshire Way

Introduction

The Concept

This book of local walks in a small part of the Chiltern Hills follows on the principle of my last book published called *The Surrey Hills*. Walkers in general seem to prefer shorter circular walks close to their home or within easy travelling distance. I have therefore tried to construct walks that present and promote the beauty of the Chilterns in day walks of easy length for both the novice and experienced walker. Those walkers who prefer longer distances can, if they wish, combine more than one walk.

The Style

Each walk is constructed to include all relevant information regarding its route

The Routes

The walks are in a southerly geographical area of the Chilterns within a triangle of the M40, the *Ridgeway* path and the A4130. This compact area has plenty of variation to offer the walker, be it forest, hills, views, valleys or villages. Some routes purposely overlap to allow walkers to mix and match walks by switching from one walk to another. The walks do not necessarily need to begin at the point the author writes, but may be started in a different location to allow stops or breaks that suits the walker better.

Photography

All but two photographs in this book were taken by the author.

N. B. Please do not be put off by the frequent use of Ordnance Survey grid references or compass bearings in this book. In the main they are extra information for those walkers who wish to make use of them. The walks can be walked without the knowledge of grid references or compass bearings.

Some Basic Information

Maps and navigational equipment

I would like to claim that every person should be able to find their way on each walk with the aid of this book. However, I would well advise each walker to always carry the appropriate Ordnance Survey map and a compass. Only one map, the Ordnance Survey Explorer 171 is required for all the walks contained in this book. I have given grid references at key points to assist those walkers who like to use their GPS navigational equipment. **It is not necessary to understand grid references to use this book.**

Clothing and equipment

It is always advisable on country walks to use ankle support boots but it is possible to do all the walks in trainers. Some walkers find that a trekking pole is useful for contemplating hills. It is useful to carry wet weather clothing at all times, or possibly a folding umbrella.

Accommodation

Should the walker need overnight accommodation I have included a list of Tourist Information Centres where this information can be obtained.

Transport

Unfortunately there is little in the way of public transport for the majority of these walks. There are buses along the main roads, the A4130 with various drop off points for Mill End, Lower Assendon, Bix, Nettlebed, and Nuffield Place; along the B482 at Lane End and Cadmore End. It is also possible to join some walks by walking from Stokenchurch. Car parks are noted where applicable. It is also worth phoning a public house for permission to use their car park in exchange for having lunch there. Lots of landlords are receptive to this idea. It is **not** advisable to use their car park for walking purposes without their prior permission.

Refreshments

Cafes, tea shops and public houses are mentioned but I would always advise walkers to carry their own supplies of food, and water particularly on hot days.

Footpaths

All footpaths in this guidebook are official paths as shown on the Ordnance Survey map (Explorer 171). They are well used by locals, ramblers, dog walkers and visitors alike. There are no problems with access on the walks described. Please bear in mind that footpaths/gates/stiles do change over time, stiles are replaced by gates, new paths appear or disappear and original paths may be re-routed, gaps appear in hedgerows or disappear, farmers may create enclosures within fields or remove them.

Safety

On occasions walks may cross roads where great care should be taken. It is always best to walk along roads where you can best be seen by other road users in both directions.

Places of interest

I have given details of historical note or places and things of interest along the walks to enliven those moments of rest. Additionally they are numbered in the information box in each walk which can be referred to for detailed notes at the back of the book.

GPS information

For the benefit of those walkers interested in gadgets I have included some Ordnance Survey grid references at many locations to enable the route to be planned, or get lost with greater accuracy. The references might prove useful for those who possess a GPS should they wish to walk the route in reverse. Having said that there is no substitute for the old fashioned map and compass; maps don't need batteries or lose a signal in a wood!

Maps within the book

The printed maps in this book are presented conventionally, North at the top. Arrows denote the described direction of the walk. They are intended to give a general idea of the route of the walk and are to scale. In the main I have chosen not to include historical locations on the maps in order to keep them uncluttered. All maps in this book were created by the author.

Walk Routes

1. Cadmore End, Turville, Skirmett, Frieth, Fingest

2. Fingest, Hanover Hill, Ditchfield, Moor Common, Frieth, Skirmett

3. Fingest, Penley Wood, Ibstone, Idlecombe Wood, Turville

4. Hambleden, Killdown Bank, Hutton's Farm, St Katherine's Convent and Skirmett.

5. Hambleden, Huttons Farm, Bottom House, Colstrope, Bacres Farm, Woodend Farm, Red Hill, Pallbach Hill, Hambleden brook

6. Henley, Henley Park, Benhams, Fawley, Fawley Bottom and Middle Assendon

7. Ibstone, Turville, Southend, Skirmett and Fingest.

8. Stoner, Bosmore Farm, Luxters Farm, Skirmett, Poynatts Wood and Kimble Farm

9. Stonor, Southend, Turville Court, Turville Grange, Pishill, Lodge Farm

10. Bix, Bix Bottom, Lodge Farm, Stonor, Cowlease Farm, Middle Assendon

11. Bix, Catslip, Upper Maidensgrove, Warburg Nature Reserve, Lodge Farm, Warmscombe Lane

12. Maidensgrove, Warburg Nature Reserve, Russell's Water, Hollandridge Farm, Pishill, Oxfordshire Way.

13. Cowleaze Wood, Ridgeway path, White Mark, Christmas Common, Wellground Farm, Lower Vicar's Farm, RAF memorial

14. Cowleaze Wood, Wellground Farm, Northend, Christmas Common, Shirburn Hill

15. Christmas Common, Ridgeway, Cookley Green, Russell's Water, Pishill, Oxford Way

16. Nettlebed, Ewelme Park, Swan's Way, Swyncombe House

17. Ewelme, Swan's Way, Ridgeway, Ewelme Park, Swyncombe Manor, Swyncombe Downs, Huntingland

18. Ewelme, Brightwell Baldwin, Britwell Salome, Ridgeway, Swan's Way

About the Author

Photo Maureen Clarkson

Leslie is a keen walker, a member of the Rambler's Association, and walks with the Staines Group. He is long retired from British Airways and of his many interests he has written three historical walking guidebooks, this being the fourth. The previous books are listed above.

After completing *The Surrey Hills* he looked around for another nearby area to put together more circular walks in a compact area. He chose the Chilterns and proceeded to research walks and local history of the area covered by his walks.

Leslie is a resident of Weybridge and first began his walking in the Surrey Hills in the 1960's. He has trekked in various parts of the world in such places as the Himalayas, New Zealand, China, South Africa, mainland France, Corsica, Madeira, Azores, Spain, Romania, Patagonia, Peru, Bolivia and Mali.

In addition to walking his other main interests include travel, photography, history, genealogy, archaeology, music, poetry, modern art, and things art deco.

Walk 1

Cadmore End, Turville, Skirmett, Frieth, Fingest

Map:	OS Explorer 171
Start/Finish points:	Cadmore End roadside parking off Marlow Rd at SU7831 9276
Distance:	14kms (8¾ miles)
Time:	3½ hrs
Transport Rail:	Marlow, Henley
Bus:	Cadmore End
Places of interest:	Cobmore Windmill, Hambleden valley, St Mary the Virgin church Turville and Turville village, Skirmett village, St John the Evangelist church Frieth and Frieth village, St Bartholomew church Fingest and Fingest village.
Refreshments:	Bull and Butcher ph Turville, The Frog ph Skirmett, The Yew Tree ph Frieth, The Chequers ph Fingest.
Local History Notes:	8, 38, 32, 19, 18
Walk description:	A four village hilly walk that offers glorious views. The walk goes through woods across valleys and visits four delightful villages.

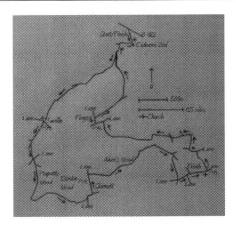

The Route

Leaving the lay-by car park walk past the common along a surfaced lane. Pass by St Mary Le Moor church on the left then walk to the right and join a track between grassy areas.

Follow this track which later swings left and down hill. Ignore the track on the right and continue on into Hanger Wood and in 30m at a Y-junction take the right-hand fork leading uphill. Just past a cross track *(not a footpath)* continue on for another 30m where there is a sign giving a map grid reference of 779 921, here turn right. In over 100m at an inverse Y-jct follow the track left passing Maggs Pond on the left and then go downhill on a grassy track. Cross over a cross track and continue downhill on a steep track to reach a gate. Go through a gate and enter Manor Farm. Walk down the steep field on its left-hand edge. Exit through a gate and go forward and cross over a step stile to join a lane, Chequers Lane *(at SU7750 9179)*, here turn right.

In 100m turn left through a gap by a wide gate and in a further 40m bear left onto a narrower track leading uphill alongside a fence on the left. At a Y-junction of tracks *(at SU7727 9168)* take the right-hand uphill track. Exit the path over a step stile and join a lane opposite a windmill, Cobstone Mill.

Here turn right and just past the windmill turn left through a kissing gate and enter a field. Go forward down its left-hand edge and then through a gap in the hedgerow. Turn immediately left and right through another hedgerow and follow the very steep track downhill towards the village of Turville. Go through a gate and continue on towards Turville. Exit through a kissing gate and go forward to reach the centre of the village. *(The Bull and Butcher ph is to the left.)*

Turville   Old school sign, Turville

Walk half right across to a surfaced lane to the left of the St Mary the Virgin lych-gate passing Sleepy Cottage on the corner *(notice the preserved old 'school' sign on the corner, depicting children complete with satchels and caps)*. Walk up the access lane and at its end go up the track in the right-hand corner. Go through a gate and continue up the right-hand edge of the field. In about 150m *(at SU7650 9074)* bear left on a track across the field on bearing about 165 degrees. Exit through a kissing gate *(Mildred's Gate, dedicated in memory of Mildred Ledbury, who loved this valley, 1914-2009)* to reach a lane.

Cross over the lane and go over the step stile opposite by a wide gate and go forward on the track ahead into woodland. Exit the wooded area and in 5m bear half-right across the field *(on bearing about 190 degrees)*. Across the field enter Poynatts Wood and keep to the track ahead. At a junction of tracks on a bend take the broad track left leading uphill. Maintain this track ignoring others which later swings left *(at SU7651 8967)* over the hill and then begins to go downhill. In a few metres at a Y-jct continue on ahead going downhill following the arrows on the trees. The broad rough track swings left again; continue downhill always keeping to the broad track. After 700m the track narrows and descends to a lane *(at SU7754 8981)*. Here turn left and follow the lane into Skirmett.

Walk on past the *Frog ph* and in 40m turn right on a track. At its end go through on the left before a residence and enter a field. Continue in the same direction and then walk across a horse gallops. Exit through a gate and continue on across another field in the same direction. Exit over a step stile on the right to join a broad track, here turn left up the broad track. At a point where it enters Adams Wood go forward up the main track ignoring others. At a broad diagonal cross *(at SU7849 9062)* there is a seat with a dedicated inscription which reads*:*

(Part of the surrounding area is dedicated in the memory of Reg Buller, beloved husband, father, writer, who travelled the world but loved Frieth best of all).

Here turn right on a downhill track. Exit Adams Wood and enter a field walking along its right-hand edge. Exit in the top right-hand corner to meet a cross track at a T-junction *(at SU7874 9072)*, here turn right.

At an un-surfaced lane junction at Frieth Court, on the left, continue ahead. The track meets a surfaced lane, continue on in the same direction and in a further 50m turn right on a track by The Cottage. Walk through their gardens exiting through a gate continuing on an enclosed track. Exit the path to join a lane.

Here turn left and in 200m arrive at a T-junction on a bend. Go forward on the road opposite into Frieth. Walk past St John the Evangelist church on the right. (*The Yew Tree ph is on the left past the church.*) Immediately past the church turn left on a track. Go through a kissing gate and walk along the left-hand side of a field. Exit in the left-hand corner through a kissing gate and go forward on an enclosed track. Exit through a kissing gate and go down steps to reach a lane, here turn left.

In about 200m just after where the lane goes right and left turn right just after *Spurgrove Cottage* on a very broad track. At a junction go forward on a narrower track to the left of wide gates and a garage. Enter Mousells Wood, ignore the track on the left, and maintain the direction downhill to reach a T-junction of tracks (*at SU7940 9087*), here turn left. At a cross track continue on ahead. Maintain this track and direction ignoring others. Exit through a kissing gate to meet a broad cross track on a bend (*at SU7871 9079*), here turn right and continue to go through a gap by a wide gate. Continue ahead across a field. Once across the field enter Fingest Wood. Continue on the track leading down to the left. Exit the wood over a step stile and walk down the left hand side of the field. Exit the field over a step stile by a gate and continue down a hilly field with a view of Fingest ahead. Go over a step stile and continue on. Exit in the left-hand corner over a step stile to reach a lane, here turn left into Fingest. (*The Chequers ph is on the left at a T-junction of lanes.*)

At a T-junction opposite *The Chequers ph* turn right up Chequers Lane passing St Bartholomew church on the left. 40m beyond the church turn right on an enclosed track. At a Y-junction by a step stile take the right fork. Go over a step stile and walk along the right-hand edge of a field and before the end of the field go over a step stile to reach a broad farm track. Turn left and continue on up the track entering Hanger Wood. At a Y-junction by a log storage hut bear left uphill. Maintain this track on the edge of the woodland ignoring others. At an inverse Y-junction maintain direction re-joining the outbound track at this point. Continue on ahead uphill ignoring other tracks. It swings round to the right and reaches Cadmore End opposite St Mary Le Moor church. Here turn left along the lane to the car park.

Walk 2
Fingest, Hanover Hill, Ditchfield, Moor Common, Frieth, Skirmett

Map:	OS Explorer 171
Start/Finish points:	Fingest village at SU7771 9114
Distance:	13kms (8 miles) inc Chapel detour
Time:	3¼ hrs
Transport Rail:	None on route
Bus:	Nearest is at Lane End 500m off route then join the walk at Ditchfield.
Places of interest:	St Bartholomew church Fingest Ditchfield village, Site of the chapel that was moved to Cadmore End
Refreshments:	Chequers ph Fingest, The Yew Tree, Frieth, The Frog Skirmett
Local History Notes:	18, 12, 25, 19, 32
Walk description:	Hills, villages, woods, valleys, site of former Chapel now moved to Cadmore End.

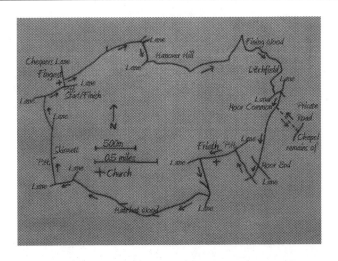

The Route

Walk away from the T-junction along Chequers Lane opposite the Chequers ph *(at SU7771 9114)*, after 60m turn right up an enclosed track. At a Y-jct of tracks take the right-hand enclosed track. Go over a step stile and walk along the right-hand edge of a field. Exit over a step stile to join a broad farm track, here turn left uphill. At a Y-jct by a barn *(at 7816 9149)* bear right. Meet a broad farm track at Hanger Estate, here turn left and follow the broad track, which emerges over a step stile into a field. Exit in the bottom right-hand corner of the field over a step stile. Continue on the right-hand edge of another field. Follow the hedgerow round to the right and exit the field through a kissing gate and then up shallow steps to meet a lane on a bend *(at SU7871 9166)*, here turn right along the lane.

The Chequers public house, Fingest

In 200m and where the lane goes sharp right *(at SU7878 9143)* turn left over a step stile into a field just before 9 Acres bungalow. Follow the track round the edge of the field. Exit over a stile and continue on ahead, *(Hanover Hill is on the left.)* Exit through a kissing gate and continue on the right-hand side of the field ignoring the track on the left. In the right-hand corner of the field follow the track round to the left. In less than 200m *(at SU7942 9138)* enter a wood through a gate. Exit the wood through a gate and continue alongside the wood. After about 200m *(at SU7977 9144)* where the track goes right, turn left through a kissing gate and continue on the track in the same direction with the wood on the left. Go through a kissing gate and continue into Fining Wood, in 5m ignore the track on the right and continue on ahead. After about 150m at an inverse Y-jct, *(at SU7998 9177)*, turn very sharp right. At a Y-jct in 200m bear left. Maintain the track through the wood ignoring others, cross over a metal footbridge and go up shallow steps. Later cross over a plank bridge. Exit through a kissing gate and walk between residences to enter the village of Ditchfield.

Here turn right down the broad unmade road. In 300m turn right and follow the broad track, which leads to a narrow path, round to a T-jct, here turn left. Go through a kissing gate and continue up to a road *(at SU8042 9104)*.

Cross over the road and turn left and in less than 100m turn right on a surfaced access lane. Then take the right fork on a track. In 200m reach a T-jct *(at SU8041 9085)*.

At this junction there is an option to visit the site of the remains of the chapel that was moved to Cadmore End. Directions are as follows:
Turn left at this T-jct and walk alongside the wall of a residence. Go through a kissing gate and continue across a field in the same direction, on bearing about 140 degrees. Exit through a kissing gate to reach a lane. Opposite the kissing gate is the location of the remains of the chapel (at SU8068 9056). Return to the T-jct the same way. Once back at the T-jct turn left and continue as below.

Omitting the diversion continue on ahead and walk on through woodland. Keep to the obvious track, marked with white arrows, ignoring others, which undulates through woodland occasionally passing residences. Cross over an access drive and continue on in the same direction. Cross over a cross track and maintain direction. Cross over a plank bridge and in 25m *(at SU8033 9035)* turn right. The track emerges to an open area and later joins an un-surfaced access drive at residences, continue on in the same direction. The drive emerges at a lane at Moor End *(at SU8019 9015)*.

Cross over the lane diagonally left and go through a gate to the left of a broad track and enter a wooded area. At a T-jct with broad track turn left along it and in 50/60 metres reach a multi track junction *(at SU8012 9000)*. Here just before junction turn right through a kissing gate and continue on the right-hand edge of a field at about 330 degrees. Exit in the right-hand corner through a kissing gate and continue on ahead across the middle of another field. Exit to a lane in Frieth village here turn left.

Walk on through the village past *The Yew Tree* ph and in 500m turn left along an access road *(Hayles Field)*. At its terminal point continue on the enclosed narrow track ahead. Exit to a broad track by a lane, continue on ahead on the broad track parallel to the lane.

Exit in the right-hand corner of a farm area through a kissing gate and cross over the lane.

Go over the step stile opposite and continue on the track ahead leading to Hill's Wood, which later becomes Hatchet Wood. Continue on path through woodland, ignoring permissive path on right. At an inverse Y-jct in Hatchet Wood *(at SU7883 8953)* turn right downhill. After 1.1kms exit reach a lane, here turn left.

Walk down the lane to a road junction on a bend, here turn right into the village of Skirmett. 300m after *The Frog* ph and just past a disused lane on left with barrier go through a gate on the left on right of disused lane and enter a field. Continue on the left hand side of the field exiting through a gate to enter another field. Cross the field half right and exit through a gate to continue in the same direction. Exit through a gate to reach a lane, here turn right and walk into Fingest. At a junction of lanes turn left into the village back to the start/finish point.

Walk 3
Fingest, Penley Wood, Ibstone, Idlecombe Wood, Turville

Map:	OS Explorer 171
Start/Finish points:	Chequers Lane, Fingest at SU7771 9112
Distance:	11.9kms (7½ miles)
Time:	3hrs
Transport Rail:	None on route
Bus:	None on route
Places of interest:	St Bartholomew church Fingest, The standing stone at Ibstone, Hell Corner Farm Ibstone, St Mary the Virgin church Turville and Turville village
Refreshments:	Chequers ph Fingest, Bull and Butcher ph Turville, Fox Country Inn Ibstone
Local History Notes:	18, 22, 39, 38
Walk description:	Woods, villages, valley views

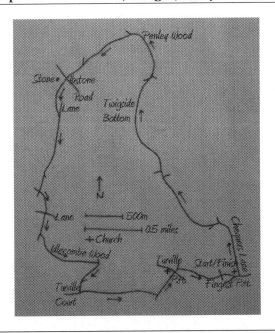

The Route

Leaving the junction in Fingest opposite the *Chequers ph* at (*SU7771 9112*), walk along Chequers Lane. After 800m or so at (*SU7741 9181*), turn left through a gap by a wide gate on to a track. In about 30m ignore the track on the left and another in a further 20m and continue on ahead on the broader track entering a wooded area; the track leads slightly uphill. Maintain a northerly direction, the path occasionally divides to avoid the wetter parts. After 1.1kms at a junction, where a broad track goes off to the right, continue on ahead on the obvious track leading north ignoring other tracks. In 300m go over a step stile by a wide gate and continue on the broad track ahead. At a Y-Jct bridleway in 400m at *(SU7629 9293)* take the right fork continuing in the same direction. Exit the track in 100m at a broad un-surfaced access track into Harecramp Estate.

Cross over the track half right and go over a step stile and follow the track ahead. The track continues on into woodland *(Twigside Bottom)* and after 800m reach a clearing and track junction at *(SU7645 9377)*. Join a track from the left and continue on in the same direction. Maintain the obvious track and after a further 600m pass under overhead cables. In a further 200m reach a clearing at a distinctive Y-Jct at *(SU7613 9438)*; bear left on bearing about 255 degrees. In about 150m the track enters a hilly field, walk along its left-hand edge. In the left hand corner of the field cross over a farm track and go forward on the track opposite entering woodland. The track later goes uphill and emerges from the wood into a large field, continue on ahead on the left hand side. Exit in the left hand corner of the field and go forward on an access drive between residences to meet a road in the village of Ibstone at *(SU7523 9374)* opposite the village cricket field.

Cross over the road and walk along the right hand edge of the cricket field and after about 100m turn right on a track leading towards a standing stone on the common *(this is the Ib-stone)*. Walk 100m to the stone. The Stone is at *(SU7509 9371)*.

Do an about turn and retrace your steps back and in 20m bear right on a grassy track on bearing about 180 degrees across the common. Once across the main common area, cross over an unsurfaced broad track and continue on the narrow track opposite. In 10m meet a wider grassy track. Here turn right and keep to this track ignoring others. Slowly bear round to the left and go slightly downhill towards woodland. Exit to a T-jct of partially un-made lanes *(at SU7514 9329)*.

Ib-stone

Here turn right and pass by residences and later Hell Corner Farm *(on the left)*. Continue along the lane to its end. Take the track to the right of the last residence and enter the wooded area of Wormsley Estate. There are two tracks leading down the hill, keep to left hand wider track. After 500m at a Y-jct at *(SU7494 9241)* bear right on the steeper downhill track. In 20m go through a kissing gate and emerge from the wooded area. Go forward down a valley slope across rough pasture. Go over a step stile and continue in the same direction across a field on bearing about 180 degrees. Go through a kissing gate and enter a wooded area. Go forward to reach a lane.

Cross over the lane and go through a kissing gate opposite, continue in the same direction up the other side of the valley towards a wooded area. Once at the top of the field go over a step stile into a wooded area. In a few strides turn left walking slightly downhill to eventually reach a surfaced access drive. Here turn right and in 15m walk past a wide electric gate to reach a lane *(Holloway Lane)* at *(SU7498 9187)*.

Walk half right across the lane, cross over a step stile and enter a field. Continue on ahead up the right-hand edge of the field towards woodland. Exit the field over a step stile and enter Idlecombe Wood up steps. At the top of the steps meet a cross track at *(SU7489 9157)*, here turn left. After 1km at a T-jct at *(SU7575 9121)* turn right uphill and exit Idlecombe Wood. At a four track junction at *(SU7547 9097)* take the second left broad track leading up over the hill. In a further 150m exit the track by a wide gate at the terminal point of a lane at Turville Court.

Here turn immediately left through a gate and walk along a broad track on bearing about 90 degrees. Go through a gate and continue on the right hand side of a field. The field narrows before a gate. Go through the gate and continue on a downhill track later bearing right and going underneath overhead cables. Continue down the field to exit through a gate at *(SU7655 9083)* to enter another field, here turn left. In 50m go through a gate and continue on the enclosed track ahead. Exit at the end of an access drive and continue on down into Turville village.

Walk half right across the green to meet a track to the right of a residence called *"The Old School House"*. Go forward through a gate and immediately turn right through a kissing gate continuing on a grassy track. Go over a step stile and continue ahead in a wooded area.

Cross over a lane and go through a gate and continue ahead. In less than 100m at a junction of tracks turn right downhill. Go through a gate to meet a lane, here turn left into Fingest.

Walk 4
Hambleden, Killdown Bank, Hutton's Farm, St Katherine's Convent and Skirmett

Map:	OS Explorer 171
Start/Finish points:	Public car park in Hambleden behind the Stag and Huntsman ph at SU7850 8659
Distance:	14kms (8½ miles)
Time:	3½ hrs
Transport Rail:	Nearest Marlow, Henley
Bus:	The walk could be joined part way round by alighting from the 800/850 bus on the A4155 at Westfield Farm (see below for directions to join the walk)
Places of interest:	Hambleden village, St Mary the Virgin church Hambleden (WH Smith brass plaque), Manor House (Lord Cardigan's birthplace), St Katherine's Convent
Refreshments:	Village shop Hambleden, Stag and Huntsman ph Hambleden, The Frog ph Skirmett (400m off route)
Local History Notes:	20, 28, 32
Walk description:	In the lower parts of the Hambleden valley this walk offers valley views, woodland, villages and farmland, some lane walking.

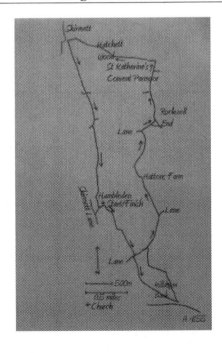

The Route

Exit the car park at the opposite end to the entrance and enter a large field. Walk across the field half left on bearing about 120 degrees towards a Manor House exiting the field through a gap in the hedgerow to a broad cross track. Here turn right passing tennis courts on the right. After 350m at a T-junction of tracks turn left. When the track enters a field turn right along its right hand edge. On approaching a wood after a dip bear right to find a hard to spot kissing gate amongst the trees. Go through the kissing gate entering the woodland and in 10m turn right through a second kissing gate to enter a field. Here turn left and walk up the field. Exit the field 40m down from the left-hand corner through a kissing gate and go forward on the left-hand edge of another field. Exit in the left-hand corner over a step stile to join a lane.

Here turn right and diagonally across the lane locate some shallow steps to the right of entrance gates. Go up steps and go through a kissing gate to enter a field. Here turn left and cross the field keeping to the upper edge of the field on bearing about 165 degrees or about 40m parallel down from the left-hand hedgerow and go forward to a step stile. Go over a double step stile and continue on in the same direction across another field. Cross over a stony farm track and continue in the same direction initially by the left hand edge of the field going slightly downhill to go through a wide gap in a tree line. Continue on along the right-hand edge of a field. Exit the field to enter a wood *(Killdown Bank)*. Continue on this narrow track to a T-junction *(at SU7987 8476)*, here turn left uphill. *(You may join the walk here if using the bus see below for directions.)*

Hambleden valley

Continue on this track for 600m exiting through a gap to enter a field. Cross the field on bearing about 290 degrees and in less than 100m continue on the enclosed track on the left of two wide gates.

The track turns right alongside a wood then descends left and down to a junction before a lane. Bear right on the narrower track and go through a kissing gate and join the lane.

Cross over the lane and go up the track opposite immediately turn right over a step stile and walk along the right-hand edge of a field parallel to the lane. In 330m turn right over a step stile to re-join the lane, here turn left along it. After less than 400m turn left along a broad farm track to Hutton's Farm. Continue on this track ignoring others and pass by the converted farm buildings. At the end of the track it goes left and in less than 100m turn right by double wooden gates on a broad track and walk along the top right-hand edge of the field. Maintain the broad track ignoring a track on the left and enter a wooded area. After 180m reach a Y-junction, here take the left-hand track leading downhill and in 30m bear right on a narrower track for 700m crossing over a cross track on the way. Exit the path over a step stile to join a lane (at SU7919 8803).

Here turn right on the lane, (Rockwell End Hill). In less than 400m turn left along Parmoor Lane walking either on the verge or banking. In 500m pass by the end of Colstrope Lane and continue on ahead. In just over 400m pass by a lane signed to Marlow on the right and continue on ahead. Pass by St Katherine's Convent Parmoor on the left and in a further 150m turn left on a broad surfaced access drive.

After passing residences on the right the drive becomes a narrower track. At a track junction take the obvious track bearing right downhill into Hatchet Wood. At an inverse Y-junction continue on the downhill track. The track emerges at a lane on a bend (at SU7786 8994).

Here turn left towards Skirmett village. Before the end of the road turn left through a gate signed (Chiltern Way), which we now follow back to Hambleden. Walk on ahead on a faint track on bearing about 150 degrees. Exit the field by a wooden gate to enter another field and walk along its right-hand edge. Exit the field by a wooden gate and cross over a farm track (Arizona Farm) and continue on through the kissing gate opposite and walk along the left-hand edge of a field. Exit the field by a kissing gate continue on ahead in the same direction. Exit through a kissing gate and continue on across another field in the same direction. Exit the field through a gate, a dedication sign attached reads (In loving memory of John Denison 1920 – 2005).

Cross over the lane and continue on the track opposite. The track emerges into a field, walk along its right-hand edge. Leaving the field in the right-hand corner continue on a broad grassy access track which joins a lane on a bend.

Here continue ahead in the same direction passing Colstrope Farm. Immediately after where the road turns right, turn left through a kissing gate and continue on ahead across a field. Exit through a kissing gate and continue on along the right-hand edge of a field. Exit through a kissing gate and continue on the left-hand edge of a field. Exit through a kissing gate and continue on the left-hand edge of another field. Exit through a kissing gate and go forward past a residence at the end of an access drive.

Cross over the drive and continue on the enclosed track opposite between residences. Go through a kissing gate and continue on the grassy track ahead. Exit through a kissing gate and go forward

through a second kissing gate to enter a field with a view of Hambleden church ahead. Continue in the same direction then veer away from the left-hand hedgerow to go through a kissing gate and across another field. Then take the right-hand faint track veering to the right. Exit through a kissing gate to a lane, here turn left into Hambleden.

Go through the churchyard of St Mary the Virgin and exit through the lych-gate. Here turn left and walk past the *(Stag and Huntsman ph)* then turn right into the car park.

Hambleden stream

Notes on joining the walk using the bus:

Coming from the Marlow direction alight from the 800/850 bus at Westfield Farm or cottages on the A4155 1½kms from Mill End. Cross over the road and walk up the path opposite at SU7996 8470. After 100m join the walk at a track junction at SU7987 8476 and continue as described in the main text at the end of the second main paragraph.

Coming from the Henley direction alight from the 800/850 bus at Westfield Farm or cottages and take the path as described in this paragraph to join the walk.

See note above at the end of the second paragraph in the main walk description to continue the walk.

For bus timings please see the useful information websites at the back of this book.

Walk 5
Hambleden, Huttons Farm, Bottom House, Colstrope, Bacres Farm, Woodend Farm, Red Hill, Pallbach Hill, Hambleden brook

Map:	OS Explorer 171
Start/Finish points:	Public car park Hambleden beyond the Stag and Huntsman ph at SU7850 8659.
Distance:	12.9kms (8 miles)
Time:	3¼ hrs
Transport Rail:	None on route
Bus:	None on route
Places of interest:	Hambleden village, St Mary the Virgin church Hambleden (WH Smith brass plaque), Manor House (Lord Cardigan's birthplace) WH Smith's Manor House.
Refreshments:	Village shop Hambleden, Stag and Huntsman ph Hambleden
Local History Notes:	20
Walk description:	A walk across valleys, through woodland, over hills offering glorious views.

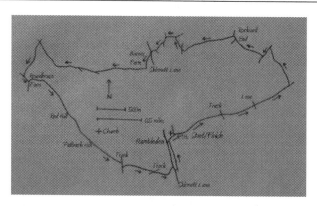

The Route

Exit the car park at the lane and turn right up a surfaced track *(signed Private Road)*. Continue up the track ignoring others, which eventually becomes unsurfaced and narrower and enters a wooded area. Continue on ahead towards the top of the hill where the track joins another from the left by a gate into a field. Ignore the track on the right and continue in the same direction up the hill also ignoring another track on the left in a further 20m.

Exit the wooded area through a gate by a wide gate and go forward passing farm buildings on the right. Continue on the broad access track ahead. At a broad cross track at Huttons farm *(at SU7926 8694)* continue ahead. At the terminal point of the surfaced track exit Huttons Farm at a lane.

Hambleden village

Cross over the lane and go through wide gates. Continue on the broad track ahead in the same direction. When the broad track goes downhill and at the bottom of the hill on a bend, look for a track on the right leading into the wooded area *(at SU8014 8726)*. Here bear right into the woodland. Go through a gap in a fence line and follow the narrow track round to the left. Cross over a narrow cross track and continue on ahead. At a track junction maintain direction ahead on about bearing 60 degrees marked as a footpath. The track goes downhill, at the bottom turn left and exit the wooded area to reach a broad track. Turn right on this track and then immediately left on bearing about 330 degrees on another broad track. At the end of the electric fence on the left meet a track from the left, continue on ahead in the same direction going over a stile by the side of a field. Go forward on the enclosed path between a fence line and a hedgerow. Continue ahead over another stile through a wooded area emerging into a hilly field. Continue on its left-hand edge in the same direction. Exit the track beside a wide gate at a lane by a residence *(Bottom House at SU8008 8813)*.

Here turn left along the lane. In less than 200m at a T-jct of lanes turn right on a lane *(signed Henley)*. At a Y-jct of lanes at Rockwell End bear right. At a T-jct on a bend ignore the lane from the left and continue in the same direction. In less than 100m turn left on a broad track into a field. Walk along its right-hand edge.

Exit the field in the right hand corner and go forward on a tunnel track underneath trees. The track eventually bends right and descends to a 4 track junction *(at SU7854 8804)*. Cross over the cross track and continue on ahead on bearing about 320 degrees still going downhill. The track exits to a lane.

Turn left down the lane, ignore the lane on the left in 50m, and continue on downhill. Pass Colstrope Farm and exit the lane at a road *(Skirmett Rd)*.

Cross over the road and go through a gate by a wide gate opposite and enter a field. Continue on a faint track half left across a field on about 230 degrees aiming for Bacres Farm buildings. Once across the field exit through a gap in the hedgerow then pass by the converted farm buildings. Continue ahead on a broad track. The track goes sharp right and uphill. Maintain this track and direction ignoring others. After 550m at a Y-jct near the top of the hill bear left, *(the right hand track goes to Built Farm only)*. At the top of the hill cross over a broad cross track and continue on ahead in the same direction. Just after going over another cross track bear left. Cross over the broad cross track *(at SU7726 8766)* and continue ahead on a very narrow track in woodland. There is an open field on the right; once you are at the other corner of the field, in about 150m, look keenly for a narrow track on the left *(at SU7712 8767)* signposted by a white arrow on a tree. Here turn left downhill on bearing about 260 degrees following another white directional arrow on a tree. On the hillside meet a cross track, here turn right. At a Y-jct take the left fork leading downhill. The track leads down to a multi track junction in a valley area *(at SU7674 8769)*.

Here turn right and walk 10m to a Y-jct junction where there are two stout trees. Take the broad track leading uphill to the left of the two stout trees. *(Looking back the approach track to this multi track junction it is now basically in line with the exit track.)* Maintain this track which slowly ascends ignoring others. Then walk alongside a valley water course. Continue on this broad track ignoring all others. Enter a tree covered tunnel track with fields on either side. After about 500m and well before the end of the track look out for a cross track *(at SU7600 8816)*, here turn left through the hedgerow and go forward across a field. Once across the field turn left and walk alongside a fence line. After 250m turn half right over a step stile and enter another field, walk along its left-hand edge. Exit through a wide gate at Lower Woodend Farm and continue ahead along its access drive. Exit the access drive to reach a lane *(at SU7569 8752)*.

Here turn left along the lane. In 200m where the lane goes right, turn left on a broad access track by the Roundhouse. Later continue on a narrower track ahead. Maintain this track and direction ignoring others looking out for white directional arrows on the trees to reach a triangular junction after about 1.2kms with a centrally positioned tree *(at SU7674 8662)*. Bear right in the same direction. In 100m at a Y-jct bear left between old gate posts. Maintain this track and direction which eventually becomes narrower and goes downhill. Eventually the track emerges onto an open grassy area. Continue on downhill to reach a broad track by red brick residences *(at SU7752 8607),* here turn right. In 100m just before wooden gates across this track turn left on another broad track. At a Y-jct maintain direction on the right-hand track. Maintain this track and direction ignoring all others. Later where the track goes downhill for a few metres, take the track on the right leading downhill to join another track, continue on ahead past residences on your right to reach Skirmett Rd.

Here turn right and walk back down the road for about 100m. Opposite a residence turn left down a broad track. In about 100m and before a bridge over Hambleden brook turn left through a kissing gate. Go forward on the faint track ahead.

Hambleden stream, Hambleden

Exit the field by the Hambleden brook and bridge through a kissing gate, here turn right and walk into the village. Walk past the church and go forward down the road passing the *Stag and Huntsman ph*. The car park is beyond and to the right.

Walk 6
Henley, Henley Park, Benhams, Fawley, Fawley Bottom and Middle Assendon

Map:	OS Explorer 171
Start/Finish points:	Oxfordshire Way, Fair Mile at SU7578 8331. Parking, Monday to Friday use the Rugby Club Marlow Rd, Sundays the Kings Road Car Park and Saturdays either the station or Southfields off Greys Rd.
Distance:	13kms (8 miles) from start point above
Time:	3¼ hours
Transport Rail:	Henley
Bus:	Henley
Places of interest:	Henley, Fawley, St Mary the Virgin Fawley, Fawley Bottom farmhouse, Middle Assendon
Refreshments:	Henley public houses and tea shops, Rainbow Inn ph Middle Assendon
Local History Notes:	21, 15, 16, 13, 1
Walk description:	Using the Oxfordshire Way then through villages, past a village church. Then a delightful hill walk with far reaching views before re-joining the Oxfordshire Way back to Henley.

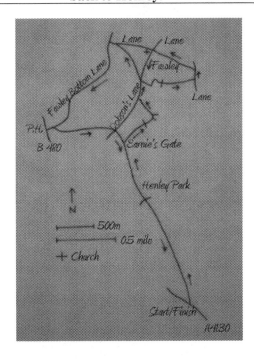

The Route

Join the walk proper at the *Oxfordshire Way* on right hand side of Fair Mile on the A4130 *(at SU7578 8331)* just beyond Rupert House playing field. Here bear right on an enclosed track the *Oxfordshire Way*. At the top of the hill the track enters woodland and bears left. Exit the woodland through a gate to enter a large field continue on ahead in the same direction on a faint track on bearing about 340 degrees and then following short marker posts. Pass by a disused kissing gate and continue on ahead. Exit through a kissing gate *(at SU7520 8469)*, here join a surfaced access drive and continue on ahead towards Henley Park.

Continue ahead past Henley Park house and other residences on the now unsurfaced broad track. After a further 600m *(at SU7495 8546)* turn right through *"Ernie's Gate"*. Continue on ahead across the field on the right hand side of a hedgerow and on the left hand

side of a field. Exit through a gate and continue ahead. In about 60m exit through another gate and cross a farm track. Go through another gate and enter a field. Walk down and up a hollow in the field on the right hand edge. Go through a gate and continue ahead. Exit through a gate and drop down to a lane.

Ernie's Gate

Cross over the lane and go through railings opposite and continue on the track ahead. Exit the enclosed track through a gate by ornate gates at a track junction *(at SU7537 8580)*, here turn left. Go through a gate by a wide gate and pass a residence continuing on the broad track ahead. After 250m reach a lane *(Dobson's Lane at SU7521 8605)*, here turn right.

After 300m at a cross track *(at SU7521 8633)* turn right on a broad gravel access track. At the terminal point of the track, before a residence, turn left over a step stile and walk round the residence.

Exit through a gate and cross over a broad farm track and continue on the enclosed track ahead between fields. At the end of the track ignore the first gate on the left. Go through the next gate where the track turns left and goes uphill. At the top of the hill at Benhams cross over an access drive and go through a wide gate and in 60m exit to a lane *(at SU7598 8632)*, here turn left.

In about 150m, just past a cottage, turn left through a tall kissing gate and go forward on the left hand edge of a field. Follow the track ahead and exit through a tall kissing gate in a tree line and continue ahead on an enclosed bushy track. The track gives way to a broad grassy track and then the terminal point of an access track which leads to a lane in Fawley, *(Dobson's Lane at SU7539 8673)*.

Here turn left and pass by St Mary the Virgin church, Fawley. After 400m and back at the point where we turned off earlier, turn right through a kissing gate and walk half right crossing a farm access track and grassy area on bearing about 340 degrees. Cross over a step stile in a fence line and continue in the same direction. Cross over a step stile in a tree line and enter a field. Walk down the field keeping to the left hand edge following the fence line. Exit through a kissing gate in the fence line to meet a broad cross track, here turn right downhill. Cross over an access drive by wide gates and continue down the track opposite. Exit over a step stile and join a lane *(at SU7488 8684)*.

Here turn left downhill and in less than 100m *(at SU7480 8686)* reach a triangular lane junction at Fawley Bottom, here turn left down the lane, *(Fawley Bottom Lane) (signed Middle Assendon 1, Henley 3)*.

Fawley Bottom Farm House

After 120m pass Fawley Bottom Farm house. Continue down the lane for 1.4kms *(nearly 1 mile)*. 50m before the end of the lane *(at SU7399 8573)* turn very sharp left up a steep track *(the Oxfordshire Way)*.

(The Rainbow Inn ph is on the main road, the B480, a further 50m further on).

Continue on the uphill track in a wooded area ignoring other tracks. Exit over a step stile to enter a hilly field, continue ahead. At the top of the hill go over a step stile, continue on an enclosed track. Go over a second step stile and go forward in the same direction across a field. Exit over a step and continue on a grassy enclosed track. Exit over a step stile to meet a lane *(Dobson's Lane at SU7486 8565)*.

Cross over the lane and continue on the track opposite. After about 250m pass by *"Ernie's gate"* on the left continue ahead re-joining the track from earlier. About 100m after Henley Park house, where the lane turns sharp left, go forward through a kissing gate and enter a large field, continue in the same direction. Maintain direction about 150/160 degrees heading south. Eventually the track descends to enter a wood through a kissing gate *(at SU7565 8374)*, continue on ahead. Later the track bears round to the right and goes downhill. Exit the track to join the A4130 which is the end/start of the *Oxfordshire Way*.

County boundary

Walk 7
Ibstone, Turville, Southend, Skirmett, and Fingest

Map:	OS Explorer 171
Start/Finish points:	Roadside parking alongside Ibstone Common in Ibstone at SU7528 9362
Distance:	14.5 kms (9 miles)
Time:	4 hours
Transport Rail:	None on route
Bus:	None on route
Places of interest:	Ibstone common, Iba-stone Ibstone, Hell Corner Farm Ibstone, St Nicholas church Ibstone, Turville church, Skirmett, St Bartholomew, Fingest
Refreshments:	Fox Country Inn Ibstone, Bull and Butcher ph Turville, The Frog ph Skirmett, Chequers ph Fingest
Local History Notes:	22, 38, 39, 33, 32, 18
Walk description:	A hilly rewarding walk passing by two churches, three villages and offering magnificent valley views.

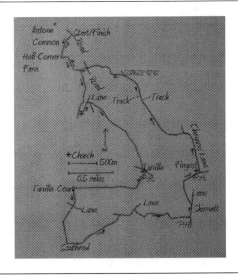

The Route

L eave the south side of the Ibstone cricket ground on a surfaced lane *(Grays Lane)* with the cricket ground on your right *(at SU7528 9362)*. After about 400m reach Hell Corner cottage on the right.

(Just beyond, on the left, is Hell Corner Farm, former home of the MP Barbara Castle). Opposite Hell Corner cottage take a track leading steeply downhill into a wooded area. At the bottom of the hill at a cross track turn right, following the white arrows on the trees. The track later slowly ascends to reach a Y-jct *(at SU7548 9295)* before an enclosed fenced track ahead, here bear right. Walk along the track a few feet below a field on the left and after about 600m turn left off the track through a gap into a churchyard. Walk past the Parish church of St Nicholas, Ibstone and exit the churchyard through a gate to join a lane.

Here turn left and in 200m at a lane junction, turn sharp right down the lane. In just over 100m bear left on a track to walk in woodland on the edge of a field on the right. Maintain this track and direction which later leaves the field and later slowly ascends through woodland. Continue to reach a track junction by a centrally positioned tree, here turn right. In a few metres turn left by a wide gate and walk along a narrow track overlooking a field on the right and offering a fine valley view. After 300m at the end of the track turn right over a step stile and enter a field. Walk half left down the field and exit over a step stile half way down the field. Go down steps entering a wooded area and exit through a gate to a field. Here turn right and in a few metres go through two gates and walk half left on a broad track leading gently downhill towards Turville. Exit through a kissing gate and go forward between residences. Go through another gate and reach a lane in Turville.

Turville village

Here turn left into the village. *(On the right is St Mary the Virgin church and beyond is the Bull and Butcher ph.)*

Immediately past the church turn right and walk up the lane passing Sleepy Cottage on the right. Continue on and beyond residences follow a wide enclosed track. Exit through a gate and ignoring the step stile on the right continue on 50m to the gate on the right. Go through the gate and maintain the faint grassy track uphill on bearing about 280 degrees. As the track gains altitude it veers round to the left underneath telephone lines and the right hand edge of the field. At the top of the hill go through a gate *(at SU7609 9084)*. Continue on ahead on the left hand side of a narrow field. Go through a gate and continue on the broad enclosed track ahead. Exit through a gate and continue along the surfaced lane ahead.

Pass by Turville Court and by its main entrance turn left through a gate *(at SU7541 9078)* and walk across a small enclosure. Exit over a step stile and continue down the left hand side of the hilly field. Exit over a step stile and go down steps to reach a lane *(Dolesden Lane)*.

Cross over the lane and go up steps and over a step stile to enter another hilly field. Walk forward to reach a valley-like depression where bear right up the depression. Towards the top of the depression bear left on an indistinct path to reach a step stile between two wide gates. Go over the step stile and walk across a small field. Go over another step stile and enter a larger field and continue on the right hand edge. Exit through a kissing gate to reach a lane in Southend, here turn left.

In a few metres at a lane junction bear left towards Southend Farm. Just past Southend Farm go over a step stile and continue along the broad enclosed farm track ahead. Exit over a step stile and continue ahead. Go over another step stile and continue down the track to meet a lane *(Dolesden Lane)*.

Here turn right, follow the lane round to the left. In a further 150m turn right over a step stile to enter woodland *(at SU7655 9048)*. Exit the wood and walk across a field in the same direction *(ignoring the track leading right)*. Enter the wooded area and in less than 100m follow the track round to the left. The track contours the hill, on the right, before bearing left downhill. The track then swings right *(affording magnificent valley views, including Skirmett to the right, Fingest middle distance and Turville to the left)*. The track then swings left. Exit over a step stile and go forward to reach a lane in Skirmett. *(The Frog ph is to the right)*.

The Frog, Skirmett

Here turn left along the lane. After about 200m and just past a disused traffic lane on left with barrier, go through a gate on the left, on right of the disused lane, and enter a field. Continue on the left hand side of the field exiting through a gate to enter another field. Cross the field half right and exit through a gate to continue in the same direction. Exit through a gate to reach a lane, here turn right and walk into Fingest.

At a road junction turn left into the village. At the T-junction with Chequers Lane is St Bartholomew church and the Chequers ph. Turn left along Chequers Lane and after 800m *(at SU7742 9182)* turn left on a track by double gates. In 50m ignore the track on the left and continue on the broad track ahead. Maintain this track for 1.6kms (1 mile) ignoring all other cross tracks. Here bear left on a track signed bridleway *(at SU7628 9292)*. Cross a cross track and continue ahead into woodland maintaining the narrow path in the same general direction. Exit to a broad track after less than 300m *(at SU7604 9302)*, here turn left to Twigside Farm.

In 100m and opposite the first farm house, bear right on a concealed track leading slightly uphill through woodland. Maintain track and direction on bearing about 265 degrees following the white arrows on the trees. Cross a farm track and continue in the same direction. Exit the wood over a step stile *(at SU7581 9306)* and go forward up a field towards a residence on the skyline. Halfway up the field bear left and right through a tree line maintaining the general direction. Exit in the top right hand corner of the field over a step stile and follow an enclosed path round to meet a road *(at SU7563 9301)*.

Cross over the road and go through a gate on to an enclosed path. Exit the path at the Y-jct *(used on the outward route earlier)*, here bear right. In about 400m turn left on an uphill track. At the top of the hill reach a lane opposite Hell Corner cottage, here turn right and in about 400m reach Ibstone cricket ground.

Walk 8
Stoner, Bosmore Farm, Luxters Farm, Skirmett, Poynatts Wood and Kimble Farm

Map:	OS Explorer 171
Start/Finish points:	Roadside parking or lay-by in Stoner village at SU7354 8839 opposite Upper Assendon Farm
Distance:	13kms (8 miles)
Time:	3hrs
Transport Rail:	None on route nearest is Henley
Bus:	None on route nearest is Lower Assendon
Places of interest:	Stoner, Luxters Farm, Skirmett
Refreshments:	The Quince Tree Stoner, The Frog ph Skirmett
Local History Notes:	34, 23, 32
Walk description:	A hilly walk, across farmland, through woodland, villages, some superb views. The author considers that the best view in this part of the Chilterns is on this walk.

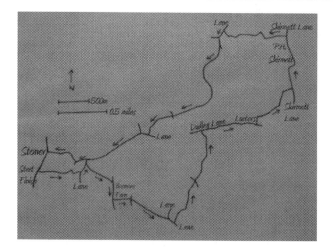

The Route

Leaving the roadside layby parking opposite Upper Assendon Farm, cross over the road and go over the stile to the right of the farm and walk up the field on the left hand side. Exit in the left hand corner and go over a step stile and continue through woodland uphill. Nearing the top of the hill meet a broad farm track on a bend, continue up the farm track in the same direction. Exiting the wood bear left towards farm buildings *(Coxlease Farm)*. Ignore the first track on the right into the farm and after passing some farm buildings meet a broad cross track, here turn right and walk into the farm proper. Go forward through a gate by a wide gate and turn left on a strip concreted access track. In just over 100m meet a lane, here turn left.

In less than 200m turn right over a step stile and enter a field. Walk across the field half right on bearing about 140 degrees. Exit over a step stile and in a few metres go over a second step stile and enter a field. Walk across the field on a faint track on bearing about 120 degrees. Exit the field through a tall kissing gate in a fence line to enter an enclosed plantation area *(Annabelles Wood),* and continue on the track ahead. Exit through a tall gate to join a surfaced access lane. Here turn right and continue on ahead passing a bar gate and then going through a kissing gate a by a wide gate. After passing a pond on the right and Bosmore Farm on the left turn left through a gate and walk round the farm initially on a surfaced track which becomes an un-surfaced track. Exit the farm buildings through a gate by a wide gate and continue on the broad track ahead. In 200m reach a junction where the farm track goes right.

Here go forward and go over a step stile by a wide gate and enter a field. Walk down the field in the general direction of the telephone poles on bearing about 120 degrees. At the bottom of the field go over a step stile and cross over a farm access track and continue on the track opposite leading uphill into woodland. The track later becomes enclosed and exits to a lane *(at SU7561 8763)*.

Here turn right and in about 100m turn left on a surfaced access drive to Lower Woodend Farm. At the farm go through a wide gate and go forward on the right hand edge of the field. Exit in the right hand corner over a step stile to enter a larger field. Walk along the left hand edge of the field by the fence line. On approaching a wide gate in the left hand corner turn right and walk across the field alongside a fence line. In the corner of the field exit over a step stile to reach a cross track *(at SU7601 8816)*. Cross over the track and go over a step stile opposite and enter a field. Continue ahead on a faint track on bearing about 40 degrees. Exit the field through a gap in the tree line and walk slightly left across another field on bearing 20 degrees. Exit the field over a step stile *(at SU7623 8852)*

and enter a woodland, continue on the track ahead. In a further
350m, after a dip in the track, walk underneath telephone lines and
go forward through a gate by a wide gate and in 50m join a lane *(at
SU7613 8891)*.

Old Luxters Farm Brewery and Vineyard

Here turn right and in about 700m pass by Luxters Farm *(at
SU7688 8901). (Luxters is a micro brewery and a vineyard and has
a cellar shop.)* In a further 200m turn left up steps and continue on
the track ahead round the edge of the vineyard. Enter a field and
walk half right down and across on bearing about 50 degrees to exit
and drop down into woodland. In 10m cross over a broad cross track
and continue on a narrow track opposite leading downhill. At a wider
cross track almost at the edge of the wood *(at SU7730 8927)* turn
right. In about 100m, before the broad track goes right and uphill,
turn left over a hard to spot step stile exiting the wooded area and
entering a hilly field. Continue down the field on the right hand edge.
Exit in the right hand corner over a step stile and follow the enclosed
track between two fields. Exit over a step stile to join Skirmett Lane,
here turn left and follow the lane into Skirmett village.

After passing *The Frog
ph*, turn left in 200m on a
broad gravel access track.
At the end of the track go
over a step stile and
continue on the enclosed
track ahead. The track
goes right

A valley view

(observe probably the best 180 degree valley view in this part of the Chilterns), then left and uphill into the woodland.

The path then takes a course to the right below the summit of the hill. Later the track contours the hill before bearing right, ignoring the track ahead, downhill to exit the wood into a field. Walk across the field in the same direction on a faint track. Once across the field enter a wooded area continue on the track ahead. Exit the wood to join a lane *(at SU7654 9045),* here turn left.

In just over 100m where the lane turns sharp right bear left on a broad track. At a Y-jct after 200m keep right. Maintain this track ignoring all side turnings for over 1km. The track later narrows before joining a broad track from a field *(at SU7582 8920),* continue on in the same direction. At a cross track *(at SU7569 8914)* continue on ahead. In a further 20m take the left permissive path towards Kimble Farm. After 400m exit the track to reach the access track to the farm, here turn left. In less than 100m reach a lane, here turn right.

After 100m ignore the lane on the right and continue on ahead for about 1km. Where the lane turns very sharp left, go forward past two wide gates on a broad track *(signed Stoner ½ mile).* In just over 200m where the broad track goes left turn right on a narrow track leading downhill into woodland. Exit the track to reach a lane in Stoner village *(at SU7368 8866).* Here turn left back to the lay-by to complete the circuit.

Walk 9
Stonor, Southend, Turville Court, Turville Grange, Pishill, Lodge Farm

Map:	OS Explorer 171
Start/Finish points:	Roadside parking in Stonor village at SU7353 8837, or further along the lane opposite the gate to Stoner Park grounds. Alternative parking can be gained in Southend village at SU7522 8975, then start the walk from there.
Distance:	11.0kms (6¾ miles)
Time:	2½ hrs
Transport Rail:	None on route
Bus:	None on route
Places of interest:	Stonor house, Stonor Deer Park, Turville Court, Turville Grange, St Paul's Pishill
Refreshments:	Crown Inn, Pishill 200m off route,
Local History Notes:	34, 33, 39, 40, 29
Walk description:	A delightful walk offering superb views of the rolling Chiltern Hills and valleys. Some hills and stiles. Lots of Red Kites.

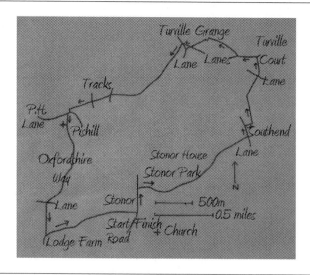

The Route

From Stonor village walk north along the road towards Stonor House. Pass by a lane on the left *(Park Lane)* and continue on for a further 200m. On approaching Stonor Park turn right

through a tall kissing gate entering Stonor Deer Park. Continue on
the track ahead on bearing about 80 degrees. Follow the faint track
which soon becomes distinctive, Stonor House is below to the left.
Continue on this track and once past Stonor House the track rises
into woodland. Maintain this track and exit Stonor Deer Park
through a tall kissing gate *(at SU7475 8931)*. Continue on the
woodland track ahead. At the top of the hill at a junction of tracks
continue on in the same direction on a broader track. Exit past a wide
gate by a residence. Go forward to reach a lane *(Drovers Lane at
SU7525 8967)*.

Here turn left along the lane and in 150m opposite a residence
named Drovers turn right along a concrete lane. In a further 150m
turn left over a step stile in the hedgerow and enter a field. Continue
ahead on the left hand side and go through a kissing gate to join a
lane.

Stonor House

Cross over the lane and go through the kissing gate opposite and
enter a field. Continue on the left hand side of the field. Exit the field
in the left hand corner over a step stile and enter another small field.
Exit over a step stile and enter a large hilly field. Ignore the track to
the left and continue half right down the dip in the field. Towards the
bottom of the field veer off to the left to a stile in the hedgerow. Exit
over the step stile to reach a lane *(Dolesden Lane)*.

Cross over the lane and go over the step stile opposite. Continue up
the right hand side of the steep field. At the top go over a step stile

and in a further 40m exit through a gate to reach a lane at Turville Court *(at SU7542 9077)*.

Here turn left and walk along the lane for 300m to a T-jct of lanes on a bend. Here turn right and go over a step stile and enter a field. Walk across the field half left on bearing about 320 degrees. In the middle of the field cross over a farm track and continue on ahead drawing closer to a hedgerow. At the hedgerow bear left alongside it. Before the end of the field turn right over a step stile in the hedgerow and enter another field. Turn left and in 100m exit over a step stile to join an access drive at Turville Grange. Continue ahead and walk round to the right in front of the house. Take the main access drive on the left leading away from the front of the house on bearing about 250 degrees. In 250m meet a road junction *(at SU7446 9094)*.

Here turn right along the road *(signed Northend 1¼ miles)*. In just over 100m reach another road junction. Cross over the road and take the footpath on the left towards a residence named *Saviours*.

On approaching its main gate take the path on the left and go through double kissing gates. Follow the main footpath in front of the house initially bearing left round a tall tree then swinging right to exit through a gate and a kissing gate then continue on ahead across another field. Exit the field through a kissing gate and continue on in the same direction. Exit this private land through a kissing gate to join a broad farm track *(at SU7404 9058)*. Here turn right continuing in the same general direction. Maintain this track for 600m to reach a hilltop with fine views then descend down to a cross track by a barn *(at SU7330 9027)*.

Plaque on seat

Go forward through a tree line and walk slightly right to continue up the left hand side of a field. After 300m exit the field by a wide gate. Cross over the surfaced cross track and go forward through a gap. Continue in the same direction down the left hand side of a field. In the bottom left hand corner exit Stonor Estate continuing on the enclosed track ahead. Go over a step stile and join a broad cross track the *Oxfordshire Way (at SU7269 9007)*. Here turn left and in 60m reach a road *(B480)* on a bend at Pishill.

Turn right along the road and in less than 100m turn left up a surfaced lane.

(Before turning left The Crown Inn ph is a further 200m along the lane on the right.)

At the top of the hill pass by St Paul's church, Pishill. Continue on ahead and before the entrance to Chapel Wells take the left of two tracks through a gap to enter a large field. *(The track is numbered PS17 and is still the Oxfordshire Way.)* Continue down the left hand side of the field and across the dip and up the other hillside heading towards a wood. At the wood cross over a cross track and continue on uphill into woodland. At the top of the hill follow the obvious track in the same general direction ignoring all others. At a Y-jct 50m before a fence line round a residence *(at SU7251 8886)*, bear left, still on the *Oxfordshire Way (signed PS17)*. The track descends to a lane *(Park Lane at SU7235 8877)*.

Cross over the lane and continue on the right hand uphill track opposite. After 250m exit the wood and go forward across a field in the same direction. Once across the field bear left alongside a hedgerow. Before reaching Lodge Farm turn very sharp left *(at SU7237 8831)* and walk back across the same field now on bearing about 70 degrees heading towards Park Wood. Exit the field over a step stile and continue ahead into woodland. The track slowly descends and in 450m exit the wood through a kissing gate *(Dedicated "In memory of Marie and Tom Barnard who enjoyed walking here")*. Walk down the hilly field initially on a faint track heading in the same direction towards Stonor on bearing about 70 degrees. Go through a kissing gate into another field and continue on ahead. Exit through a kissing gate and go forward on an enclosed track to join a road in Stonor *(at SU7367 8864)*.

Walk 10
Bix, Bix Bottom, Lodge Farm, Stonor, Cowlease Farm, Middle Assendon

Map:	OS Explorer 171
Start/Finish points:	Bix village near the church at SU7282 8519
Distance:	10.5kms (6½ miles)
Time:	2¾ hrs
Transport Rail:	Nearest is Henley
Bus:	Bix (on the A4130)
Places of interest:	Victorian water tank Bix, Ruins of old St James church Bix Bottom, St James church Bix, Stonor House.
Refreshments:	Rainbow Inn Middle Assendon
Local History Notes:	2, 3, 34, 1
Walk description:	Villages, hills and views

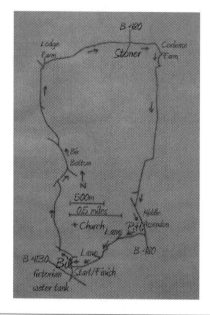

The Route

L eave the village on the lane to the left of the church passing the village hall car park on the right. In a further 100m where the lane goes sharp right, turn left on a broad track. In about 100m go forward into a field and in a further 250m at a cross track *(at SU7261 8555)* turn right on bearing about 360 degrees. Once across the field enter woodland and continue on the obvious track through the woods noticing and following the white arrows on the trees. In just over 200m at a track junction bear right on the broad track on bearing about 340 degrees still following the white arrows. The track begins to go downhill and joins a broad track, continue downhill in the same direction. Where the broad track goes right into a field continue on ahead on a narrower track near the edge of woodland. Exit the wooded area through a kissing gate to a glorious valley view *(at SU7266 8647)*. Continue down the right hand edge of the steep field. Exit in the right hand corner to join a farm cross track, here turn right towards Valley End Farm buildings. On approaching the farm go forward through a gate by a wide gate, go forward to reach a lane at Bix Bottom *(at SU7276 8672)*, here turn left.

After about 300m there is a track on the left that leads to the original Norman St James church, Bix Bottom.

The original Norman St James church, Bix Bottom

Continue along the lane for a further 100 and turn right on a broad uphill enclosed bridleway. In 200m enter woodland and the outer reaches of Warburg Nature Reserve, continue ahead. At the very top of the hill at an inverse Y-jct *(at SU7230 8769)* continue on the broad track ahead in the same direction. After 600m reach the terminal point of a farm access lane at Lodge Farm, here turn right.

In 20m turn left on a broad enclosed track. The track narrows and exits into a field. Immediately at a Y-jct bear right and cross the field heading towards woodland on about 70 degrees. Once across the field enter woodland *(at SU7263 8840)* at a stile and continue on the track ahead.

The track slowly descends through the wood and exits through a kissing gate *(at SU7302 8858)* to a superb valley view overlooking Stonor village and Stonor House. Continue on ahead down the field in the same direction towards Stonor on bearing about 80 degrees. At the bottom of the field go through a kissing gate, continue across another field in the same direction. Exit the field through a kissing gate and continue between residences to join a lane in Stonor *(at SU7368 8864)*.

Here turn left and in 20m turn right on a bridle way. The track goes uphill and round to the right and meets a farm track on a bend, here turn right towards Coxlease Farm. Walk on through the farm between two barns exiting through a gated area, here turn right on a broad track passing in front of the farm house. The enclosed farm track later emerges into a field, continue on the right hand edge of the field. After 1.5kms the track swings right and down hill. In 100m go over a step stile and continue down a winding track through woodland. After 500m exit the wooded area at a T-jct with wide farm track, here turn right. Walk down across a field exiting through or by a wide gate to join a road, here turn left.

Rainbow Inn, Middle Assendon

Walk on the lane or grass verge into the village of Middle Assendon. Immediately past the Rainbow Inn ph turn right on a broad grassy track. In less than 100m go over a step stile into a field, continue in the same direction. Exit the field over a step stile and go forward on an enclosed track. At the top of the track go over a step stile and go forward 25m to reach White Lane.

Here turn left uphill. At the top of the hill where the lane turns very sharp right at Bix Common Field take the footpath ahead across the field aiming for the church on bearing about 240 degrees. Nearing the church keep left to reach Bix village.

Victorian water tank, Bix

Directions to the Victorian water tank:
From the Bix village walk back to the A4130. Cross over the busy road and go down the lane opposite. The tank is immediately on the right.

Walk 11
Bix, Catslip, Upper Maidensgrove, Warburg Nature Reserve, Lodge Farm, Warmscombe Lane

Map:	OS Explorer 171
Start/Finish points:	Bix village near the church at SU7282 8519
Distance:	12.2 kms (7½ miles)
Time:	3 hrs
Transport Rail:	Nearest station is Henley
Bus:	Bix (on the A4130)
Places of interest:	Bix Victorian water tank, ruins of St James church Bix Bottom, St James church Bix, Warburg Nature Reserve, Bix Common Field
Refreshments:	Five Horseshoes ph Upper Maidensgrove, Rainbow Inn Middle Assendon (off route see note below).
Local History Notes:	2, 24, 44
Walk description:	Villages, woodland, hills, valleys, views and a nature reserve

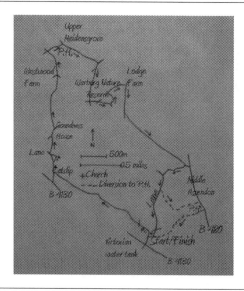

The Route

Leave the village on the lane to the left of the church passing the village hall car park on the right. In a further 100m where the lane goes sharp right turn left on a broad track and in about 100m continue ahead across a field.

Once across the field the track swings into broad woodland, continue on ahead. At a cross track continue on ahead maintaining direction. In a further 2.0kms the track joins the terminal point of an access drive at Halfridge, continue on ahead. In less than 100m at a Y-jct take the left hand broad track *(signposted track only)*. At a cross track of surfaced lanes at the Catslip *(at SU7091 8644)* here turn right along the lane walking due north.

St James church, Bix

Pass by residences and continue on ahead on the narrow lane. Beyond the dip in the lane at a Y-jct bear right. The lane later swings left past an open green area and in just over 200m *(at SU7084 8689)* at a triangular junction of lanes turn right on a footpath *(signed Russell's Water 1½)*. Go over a step stile and enter a field and walk half left on a faint track on bearing about 10 degrees. Exit through a gate to join a lane, here turn right.

In 125m at the entrance gate to *(Soundness)* at track junctions turn left on a broad track *(signed Russell's Water)*. Where the broad track goes right continue on ahead into a field walking up the right hand edge on bearing about 360 degrees. Once over the hill and in a further 80m turn right through a kissing gate set back in the tree line *(at SU7083 8797)* and walk downhill just within a wooded area on the right and a field on the left. Go through a gate and enter a field walking half left on a faint track on bearing about 340 degrees. Continue down this dome shaped field into a valley, soon a stile and a track comes into view. At the bottom of the hill go over a step stile *(at SU7097 8841)* to meet a three track junction at Westwood Farm. Here go forward on the broad track opposite *(signed bridleway)* proceeding in a northerly direction on bearing about 10 degrees.

After 600m *(at SU7076 8890)* turn right through a kissing gate and walk up the left hand side of a steep field. Exit through a kissing gate and go up shallow steps and continue on ahead. Exit the track to join a lane at Upper Maidensgrove *(at SU7107 8906)*.

Here turn right along the lane and in 100m reach the *Five Horseshoes ph.* In a further 700m *(at SU7180 8866)* where the lane swings left turn right on a broad track on bearing about 220 degrees *(signed restricted by-way Chiltern Way)*. Maintain this downhill track ignoring others, later entering Warburg Nature Reserve. After 800m *(at SU7161 8792)* reach a four track junction. Here turn left on bearing about 80 degrees. Continue on ahead for just over 400m to reach the entrance to a car park *(at SU7204 8787)*. On the right is the Wildlife Trust Visitor Centre.

Warburg Nature Reserve

Here turn left and walk through the car park exiting through a gate by a small hut. Continue on the grassy track and bear right uphill. In 200m emerge to follow the broad grassy track ahead. In 100m at a cross track turn right uphill into woodland and in 40m exit through a gate. Continue on this track uphill through a fence *(ignore sign to right)* continue uphill until you reach the exit of the Nature Reserve. Go through a gate to meet the *Oxfordshire Way (at SU7231 8824)*.

Here turn right downhill on bearing about 180 degrees. After 600m at a Y-jct *(at SU7230 8768)* bear left. Maintain this downhill track for 1.6kms, *(1 mile)* to reach a track junction at *(SU7353 8668 do not go as far as the road)*.

Here turn very sharp right on a broad farm track on the left side of a hilly field. Follow the track over the hill and round the field to reach a lane by residences *(at SU7307 8649)*.

Here turn left along the lane and in 300m reach a Y-jct of lanes.

(At this point should you wish to include the Rainbow Inn ph at Middle Assendon within your walk please see the boxed details below for directions.)

To continue the walk back to the car park, here bear right *(road signed Bix)*. In 800m at a T-jct of lanes go forward and walk across Bix Common half right aiming for the church to reach Bix village.

The directions to the Rainbow Inn from the Y-jct referred to above are as follows:

Bear left along the lane for 1km to reach the B480. Here turn right, the Rainbow Inn ph is on the right.

The route back to Bix is as follows:
Immediately past the Rainbow Inn ph turn right on a broad grassy track. In less than 100m go over a step stile into a field, continue in the same direction. Exit the field over a step stile, go forward on an enclosed track. At the top of the track go over a step stile and go forward 25m to reach White Lane. Here turn left uphill. At the top of the hill where the lane turns very sharp right at Bix Common Field take the footpath ahead across the field aiming for the church on bearing about 240 degrees.

The net difference in this diversion is plus 1.2kms (¾ mile).

Directions to the Victorian water tank:
From the Bix village walk back to the A4130. Cross over the busy road and go down the lane opposite. The tank is immediately on the right.

Walk 12
Maidensgrove, Warburg Nature Reserve, Russell's Water, Hollandridge Farm and Pishill

Map:	OS Explorer 171
Start/Finish points:	Roadside parking alongside the common on Park Lane, Maidensgrove at SU7197 8874
Distance:	13kms (8 miles)
Time:	3½ hrs
Transport Rail:	None on route
Bus:	None on route
Places of interest:	Warburg Nature Reserve, Russell's Water village and pond, St Paul's Pishill.
Refreshments:	Five Horseshoes, Maidensgrove (500m off route), Crown Inn, Pishill (200m off route)
Local History Notes:	24, 44, 31, 29
Walk description:	Hills, Nature reserve, valleys, woodland and villages

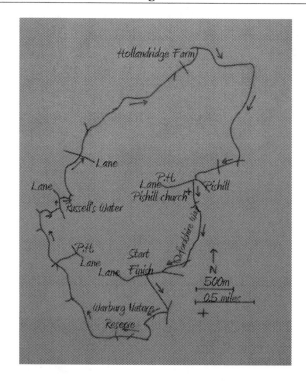

The Route

From the common on Park Lane, Maidensgrove *(at SU7197 8874)* walk diagonally left across the common in a southerly direction to meet a broad path from the left in front of residences. Continue on ahead in the same direction. In less than 100m the track joins another broad track at a small triangular junction. Continue on in the same direction now on a surfaced access. In a further 250m reach a junction at Lodge Farm *(at SU7232 8827)*.

Here bear right down a narrower track. In 20m turn right through a kissing gate to enter Warburg Nature Reserve. Continue down the path and at a Y-jct take the right hand of two tracks passing between two gates. Follow the track downhill through an avenue of trees to exit through a gate. Continue downhill for a further 40m to reach a broad green track then turn left. Follow the path round to the right through woodland. At a track junction turn left and in 30m go through a gate by a notice board in a hut. Go through the gate and through the car park to join a broad cross track in front of the Visitor Centre *(at SU7203 8786)*.

Here turn right on the broad track. After about 250m at a broad cross track continue ahead in the same direction keeping to local track signed *(SW 28)*. Continue on this track ignoring all others later exiting the Warburg Nature Reserve. Continue ahead on the narrower track. At a T-jct before Westwood Manor Farm *(step stile on the left at SU7097 8841, do not cross)* turn right. After 600m reach a cross track *(at SU7076 8890)*.

The Five Horseshoes ph
At this point the Five Horseshoes ph is 500m off route. Turn right through a kissing gate and walk up the left hand side of a steep field. Exit through a kissing gate and go up shallow steps and continue on ahead. Exit the track to join a lane at Upper Maidensgrove (at SU7107 8906). Here turn right along the lane to reach the Five Horseshoes ph. Return to the main track the same way and then turn right to continue.

Continue ahead and maintain this track ignoring all others for 800m to reach a Y-jct of tracks *(at SU7052 8958)*. Here take the right hand track leading uphill on bearing about 50 degrees. Exit the path to join a lane at Russell's Water *(at SU7084 8967)*, here turn left along the lane.

Walk past the village pond and turn immediately right and walk round the pond. Walk on and turn left immediately past a residence surprisingly named *Pond Cottage*. In less than 50m take the track to the right of residences. In a further 30m where the main track goes left into a residence go forward on a narrow track between trees to enter a large field *(at SU7098 8987)*. Here turn left on a faint track. Keep to the left hand side of the field and walk into the neck of the field taking the left of two tracks just before entering into a wooded area *(at SU7092 9013)*. Continue walking down through woodland following the white arrows on the trees exiting at a lane at *Glade House (at SU7113 9038).*

Here we temporarily leave the Chiltern Way path. Cross over the road and continue on the permissive track into woodland. Follow this steepish track uphill which goes round to the right keeping a fence on your right hand side. Once at the top of the hill there is a wide gate in the fence line, here walk left for 15m to re-join the Chiltern Way *(at SU7114 9061)*. Here turn right on a broad track. In just over 100m at a Y-jct *(at SU7120 9068)* take the right hand track which leads straight on *(locally signed as W21)*. In a further 200m at a small valley dip and a cross track, continue ahead in the same direction keeping sight of the white arrows on the trees. At a cross track *(at SU7168 9106)* continue on ahead following local track signs as W21 or CW. In a further 50m at another cross track continue on ahead uphill following the white arrows. At a Y-jct maintain the uphill track following the white arrows.

Eventually reach a small clearing *(at SU7226 9130)*. Here leave track W21 and take the hard to spot third track on the left *(locally signed PS 8 and CW)* on bearing about 50 degrees leading steeply uphill. At the top of the hill at an inverse Y-jct of tracks turn left and in 30m go over a step stile exiting the woodland. Continue on ahead across the side of a hill. Exit the field over a step stile *(at SU7259 9159)* to reach a broad cross track.

Cross over the track and continue into the field opposite and walk along its right hand edge alongside a hedgerow. At the end of the hedgerow continue ahead downhill across the field. Once across the field enter Fire Wood. In 150m meet a track junction *(at SU7279 9179)*, here turn right on a broad track on initial bearing of about 100 degrees.

At a farm cross track continue on ahead. The track goes to the right round the edge of a fenced field. Pass by farm buildings and continue on ahead to gain open valley views.

Valley view

Go over a step stile by a wide gate and continue on the left hand edge of a sloping field. Ignore the first gap in the tree line on the left and go through the second gap later. The track goes left and right through the tree line, continue on the right hand edge of another field. Exit through a wide gap and continue on the right hand edge of another hilly field.

After 150m reach a cross track *(at SU7331 9027)*. Here turn right and go forward through a tree line *(barn on left)* and walk slightly right to continue up the left hand side of a field. Exit to the left of a wide gate. Cross over the surfaced cross track and go forward through a gap. Continue in the same direction down the left hand side of a field. In the bottom left hand corner continue on the enclosed track ahead. Go over a step stile and join a broad cross track *(the Oxfordshire Way at SU7269 9007)*. Here turn left and in 60m reach a road *(B480)* on a bend at Pishill.

Turn right along the road and in less than 100m reach a T-jct on the left.

The Crown Inn
At this point the Crown Inn is a 200m detour further along the lane on the right hand side. Return the same way.

Turn left up the access lane and pass by St Paul's church, Pishill. Continue on up the lane and pass the entrance to the Old Vicarage. In less than 100m where the main track goes into Chapel Wells bear left on a track and immediately take the left of two tracks locally marked PS17, still the *Oxfordshire Way*.

The Crown Inn, Pishill

Go through a wide gate and continue on down the left hand side of the field. Go through another wide gate and continue down the field. Go down the dip and up the other side and reach a cross track before woodland *(at SU7273 8927)*, continue ahead on the path opposite leading uphill. Continue through the woodland on the obvious path to reach a Y-jct *(at SU7247 8885)*. Here take the right hand fork leaving the *Oxfordshire Way* and now following local path signed PS 19. Exit the path to reach the terminal point of an access drive by residences. Continue ahead and exit to a lane *(Park Lane at 7220 8878)*.

Here turn right to regain the car park area by the common.

Walk 13
Cowleaze Wood, Ridgeway, White Mark, Christmas Common, Wellground Farm, Lower Vicar's Farm, RAF Memorial

Map:	OS Explorer 171
Start/Finish points:	Cowleaze Wood car park north of Christmas Common at SU7257 9563
Distance:	15.8kms (10 miles)
Time:	4 hrs
Transport Rail:	None on route
Bus:	None on route
Places of interest:	Ridgeway path, White Mark, House with gravestones, RAF Memorial
Refreshments:	Fox and Hounds, Christmas Common
Local History Notes:	11, 42, 9, 43
Walk description:	A hilly walk with views, woods and interesting local history

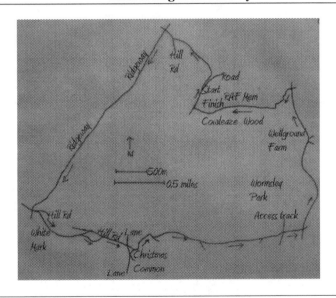

The Route

Walk to the northern end of the car park towards an open space. Here turn left and cross over the road. Turn right along a bridleway parallel to the road. Later the path becomes surfaced. At a point where the path begins to narrow at *(SU7286 9618)* turn left through a gate and continue down the right hand side of a field overlooking the Oxfordshire countryside and the M40 ahead. In 60m ignore the gate on the left and continue down a track between tree lines. Go through a gate and continue on the downhill grassy track. Towards the bottom of the hill at a fence line ignore the gates on the left and go through the right hand gate *(locally signed path L14)* and continue down the right hand side of a field. Exit through a gate at Hill Farm to join a surfaced access lane, continue ahead. In a further 200m *(at SU7209 9689)* reach a broad cross track, here turn left along the *Ridgeway*.

Continue ahead for 3kms and cross over the surfaced *Oxfordshire Way* path *(at SU7032 9454)*. Continue ahead and in a further 800m reach Hill Rd *(at SU6984 9398)*.

The White Mark

Here turn left leaving the *Ridgeway*, cross over the road in 30m, go up the narrow footpath leading uphill on the right hand side. At a junction take the middle track through a kissing gate and continue on uphill to emerge into a grassy clearing. Continue uphill and walk to the left of the *White Mark*. Right at the top of the hill veer to the left on bearing about 100 degrees. Maintain the grassy track across the top of the hill with far reaching views to the left. Exit through a gate to join a footpath leading into woodland. Cross over an access drive and continue on the path opposite. Exit to enter a car park. Walk through the car park and take the footpath on the left and meet Hill Rd and turn right. Continue along the road to reach a triangular T-jct.

Here turn right and in a further 150m reach a second triangular Y-jct.

The Fox and Hounds ph is 100m along the lane to the right.

The old village church that is now a residence complete with gravestones is a further 200m along the lane on the left.

At this junction turn left on a broad grassy track, or if you have visited the public house or church you need to return and turn right onto this path which is on bearing about 40 degrees. The track goes round to the right and at a Y-jct turn left in front of a residence. Continue on past the house and down the access drive. When the access drive goes sharp left turn right on a track *(locally signed PY3)*.

Follow the obvious track through the woodland guided by the white arrows on the trees. At a junction of tracks bear right on the track now *(locally signed SH4)* going slightly downhill. At a Y-jct continue to follow the left track *(locally signed SH4)*. Maintain this broadish track which meanders down through woodland still showing white arrows on the trees. At a track junction *(at SU7261 9344)* continue on ahead on SH4. Pass by a 10 foot high ornament *(known as the "urn"at SU7355 9349)* and a *"ha ha"* on the left. Continue on the track opposite still on track SH4. *(At SU7377 9352)* reach a surfaced access drive.

Here turn right and in 30m turn left through a gate and continue ahead across the corner of a field on a faint track. Exit through a gate and meet an access lane to Wormsley Park *(no public access)*.

Cross over the lane go through a gate and continue across a larger field in much the same direction on bearing about 70 degrees. Exit through a gate to meet a cross track *(at SU7425 9362)*.

Here turn left and continue on ahead. Exit the enclosed path at an inverse Y-jct. Continue ahead on the right hand side of a field. Exit the field and continue on ahead on a broad track. The track meets an access lane on a bend, continue on ahead. Continue past Wellground Farm and just past a residence on the left bear left on a track *(at SU7432 9526)*.

Keep to this track ignoring all others which slowly gains altitude. After 900m reach a cross track *(at SU7416 9588)*. Here turn left downhill on a narrow path *(locally signed L23)*. Go over a step stile exiting the wooded area and walk half left downhill.

Go through a tall gate in a fence line and walk round the edge of a garden at Lower Vicar's Farm. Exit through a tall gate to meet a surfaced access drive, here turn left.

In 50m turn right through the hedgerow and a gate to enter a hilly field. Continue ahead up the hill on a faint track, go through a gate in a fence halfway up the field and continue on. At the top of the hill go through a kissing gate and enter woodland, go forward still on track L23 following the white arrows.

(At SU7290 9570) is roughly the turn off point to visit the RAF Memorial.
It is in the woodland on the right hand side, you can catch sight of the stone or notice board less than 100m away. Return to the track to continue on.

RAF Memorial, Cowleaze Wood

Continue on this track L23 and cross over a cross track underneath telephone wires. In a further 100m reach Cowleaze Wood car park opposite the main entrance.

Walk 14
Cowleaze Wood, Wellground Farm, Northend, Christmas Common, Shirburn Hill

Map:	**OS Explorer 171**
Start/Finish points:	**Cowleaze Wood car park north of Christmas Common at SU7257 9563**
Distance:	**12.3 kms (7½ miles)**
Time:	**3½ hrs**
Transport Rail:	**None on route**
Bus:	**None on route**
Places of interest:	**RAF Memorial, Northend village, House with gravestones Christmas Common, Shirburn Hill.**
Refreshments:	**Fox and Hounds ph Christmas Common**
Local History Notes:	**11, 27, 9**
Walk description:	**A delightful woodland and valley walk offering fine distant views of Oxfordshire. Some hills and stiles. Lots of Red Kites.**

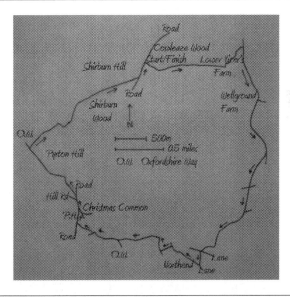

The Route

From the main entrance into the car park turn around and walk down the track opposite. Cross over a cross track underneath telephone lines and continue on the track opposite.

In about a further 300m *(at SU7290 9570)* is the turn off left to see the RAF memorial, return to the main path the same way and continue on eventually exiting the wood at a kissing gate *(at SU7346 9558)*. Go through the kissing gate and enter Wormsley Estate.

Walk forward on a faint track down the field at about 90 degrees *(the tall communications tower is on your left)*. Exit the field through a gate to join an access lane, here turn left. After 60m and before reaching Lower Vicar's Farm proper look for a tall gate on the right. Here turn right through the gate and walk round the back of the farm house. Exit through another tall gate and continue up the diagonally left track uphill amongst woodland. Before the top of the hill reach a broader cross track *(at SU7416 9588)*. Here turn right on bearing about 170 degrees.

Continue ahead towards Wellground Farm for 900m slowly descending to reach a surfaced access road *(at SU7441 9502)*. Here turn right along the road. Where the access road goes right continue on the broad unsurfaced track ahead. Later the track enters a field, continue along its left-hand edge. Once across the field bear right at a Y-jct taking the lower level track. After 600m at a cross track continue on ahead. In a further 400m leave the grassy track and go forward on a broad farm track in the same direction. Continue on to reach a lane *(at SU7416 9322)*.

Cross over the lane half-left and continue on a narrower track leading uphill between tree lines. At an inverse Y-jct meet a lane on a bend, continue on the lane in the same direction. When the surfaced lane runs out, continue ahead on an unsurfaced track still going uphill. Exit Wormsley Estate through a gate and go forward on the broad track ahead to reach a triangular road junction in Northend.

Go forward along the road *(signed Turville Heath 1¼ miles)* passing the village pond on the right. Continue on and pass the village green to reach another road junction. Here turn right on an access lane *(signed Northend Common Only)*. Continue along the lane passing residences and in 600m turn left on an enclosed track *(signed Chiltern Way at SU7298 9269)*. Exit into a field and proceed half-left down hill. Go over a step stile half way down the field and continue on in the same direction to meet a cross track *(at SU7280 9257)*. Here turn right and continue to the right-hand corner of the field. Exit the field and continue on a broad track turning left in less than 100m round Launder's Farm converted buildings.

In less than 100m where the track goes right, go forward over a step stile into a small field, continue on the left-hand edge. Exit over a step stile and enter a larger field continuing on the left-hand edge. Exit over a step stile and enter a third field continuing on the left. Go over another step stile, enter another field exiting over a step stile *(at SU7244 9278)*. Go forward into a wooded area on bearing about 270 degrees. Maintain this track which slowly descends to reach an inverse Y-jct with the *Oxfordshire Way (at SU7210 9277)*. Here turn right maintaining the same direction. Continue uphill through woodland to reach a cross track opposite Queen Wood Farm *(at SU7182 9277)*, here turn right. In less than 200m turn left on a broad track and in a further 20m turn right through a wooded area. Follow the obvious track *(white arrows on trees)* and exit the wood to meet a lane at Christmas Common. *(Just to the left is the house with gravestones.)*

Walkers stop for a thirst quencher, Christmas Common

House with gravestones, Christmas Common

Here turn right along the lane and in 150m pass by the Fox and Hounds public house. Continuing on the lane reach a triangular road junction, here go forward to a second triangular road junction in a further 100m. About 60m beyond the junction turn left on a track.

Go through a gate and enter a field and continue on the left-hand side of the field. Enter another field, ignore the gate in the hedge and after 50m the track veers off to the right at about 340 degrees. Go through a gate and meet a cross track, here turn left downhill. The track descends to meet the end of a lane at Pyrton Hill House, continue on ahead. In a further 300m *(at SU7064 9424)* turn right through a gate leaving the *Oxfordshire Way*. At an inverse Y-jct continue on ahead. Later the path goes right then later left round the edge of a field and Shirburn Wood. Exit the track through a gate and go forward down a dip and then half-right up Shirburn Hill. Go through a gate close to the top of the hill and go forward a further 100m to a cross track.

Shirburn Hill

Cross over the track and go over a step stile and enter a field. Continue in the same direction to the opposite corner of the field on a faint track on bearing about 75 degrees. Exit the field to join a road *(at SU7243 9537)*.

Here cross over the road and turn left to walk along a path in the woodland to reach Cowleaze Wood car park.

Walk 15
Christmas Common, Ridgeway, Cookley Green, Russell's Water, Pishill, Oxfordshire Way

Map:	OS Explorer 171
Start/Finish points:	Christmas Common, Hill Rd car park at SU7099 9356
Distance:	15.3kms (9½ miles)
Time:	3¼hrs
Transport Rail:	None on route
Bus:	Nearest bus is at Watlington 1 km from the Hill Rd/Ridgeway cross track where the walk can then be started from.
Places of interest:	House with gravestones Christmas Common, Village pond Russell's Water, Tumulus, St Paul's Pishill.
Refreshments	Fox and Hounds Christmas Common, Five Horseshoes Upper Maidensgrove (700m off route), Crown Inn Pishill.
Local History Notes:	9, 10, 31, 29
Walk description:	A woodland walk using the Oxfordshire Way, Ridgeway/Swan's Way, through villages, past tumulus, a church and through farmland.

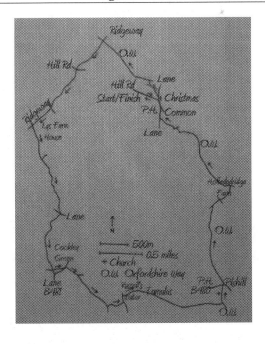

The Route

Leave the car park at Christmas Common and join the road *(Hill Rd)*, turn right and walk 300m up to the road junction. (*The Fox and Hounds ph is located by turning right for 100m at this junction.)* At the triangular junction turn left on a road *(signed Stokenchurch)* joining the *Oxfordshire Way*. In 40m turn left again on a footpath. Go through a kissing gate and enter a large field. Walk along its left-hand edge. Go through a gap and continue into another field along its left-hand edge. In less than 100m ignore the path on the left and continue round the edge of the field on a grassy track leading downhill into a wooded area. Go through a kissing gate and join a broad cross track, here turn left downhill. Continue down the edge of woodland with far reaching views to the right. The track descends to meet the end of a surfaced access drive, continue on ahead past Pyrton Hill House. In a further 700m reach the *Ridgeway/Swan's Way (at SU7032 9454),* here turn left. Maintain this broad track for 700m ignoring others to reach Hill Rd.

Cross over the road half left and continue on the broad track opposite. Continue on the *Ridgeway* to the B480 at Icknield House, on the left.

Cross over the road and continue on the lane opposite, *(signed to Dame Alice Farm). (To the left of the road in the field is a permissive footpath parallel to the lane.)* After 500m at a junction of tracks *(at SU6902 9289 Lys Farm House),* turn left off the *Ridgeway/Swan's Way* onto a surfaced lane. The surfaced access lane goes slightly uphill and later becomes un-surfaced and narrower. Maintain this uphill track later into woodland ignoring all others. After 1.6kms *(1 mile)* the track emerges at Woods Farm access drive *(at SU6958 9141),* here turn left and walk up to a road.

Cross over the road and go forward on the surfaced lane opposite *(signed to Cookley Green and Coates Farm).* Pass by Coates Farm on the right and continue on ahead. On approaching Cookley Green at the end of a row of residences at the Green, bear left across the Green to cut off the corner. Walk parallel to the private road on the left and up to the B481.

Cross over the road and turn left and in 30m turn right down a broad track by Cookley House *(at SU6975 9029)*. Beyond the residences the track narrows, continue ahead. After just over 1km at a T-jct *(at SU7053 8958)* turn left uphill. In a further 300m the track emerges at a lane in the village of Russell's Water, here turn left. *(The Five Horseshoes ph is 700m to the right at this point)*

Village pond at Russell's Water

Walk right round the village pond to the other side keeping it on your right and continue back down a broad unsurfaced access drive and in a few metres turn left *(signposted Pishill)*. Then keep right and walk away from residences and go forward on a narrower track and in about 100m exit into a large field. Cross the field half-right on bearing about 60 degrees. Walking across the field bear right aiming for farm buildings and a farm house amongst trees, *(here there is a Tumulus marked on the OS map)*. Aim for the old farm buildings, go through a wide gate *(at SU7137 8985)* and continue between the old barns on a broad track. Go forward on a narrower track into a wooded area. Maintain this track ignoring others and walk on the right-hand edge of Long Wood. After 1.4 kms *(just less than 1 mile)* at an inverse Y-jct meet the *Oxfordshire Way (which we follow back to Christmas Common)*, here turn left and in 5m join a broad access track, continue on ahead. Pass by St Paul's church Pishill and continue downhill. Meet the B480 *(at SU7267 9002)*, here turn right. *(The Crown Inn ph is 200m to the left.)*

In 60m turn left on a broad track before Pishill farmhouse. Walk on into a valley field walking to the left of a fence line. At the top of the valley after 800m the track enters woodland. In 10m bear right on an uphill track. In 50m at a Y-jct bear right again on a steep uphill track. The track emerges from the wood at a step stile, continue across the field half-right on a faint track. Exit the field in the right-hand corner over a step stile by a wide gate, here meet a broad cross track.

St Paul's church Pishill

Go over the cross track and continue on the right-hand edge of the field opposite, with a hedge on the right. At the end of the hedgerow continue ahead downhill across the field. Once across the field enter Fire Wood. In 100m meet a track junction, here turn left on the broad track which sweeps away to the right. In about 600m *(at SU7233 9218)* at a Y-jct, at a small open space on the right, take the right-hand lower level fork still on the *Oxfordshire Way*. After 700m at an inverse Y-jct by a centrally positioned tree, continue on in the same direction. The uphill track exits to a broad access drive opposite the entrance to Queen Wood Farm, here turn right.

In less than 200m at a cross track turn left by a residence. In 20m fork right into a wooded area and continue on the obvious track into an area of tall close trees. At a Y-jct keep to the left track. Exit the track to join a lane, *(to the left is a residence, once a church, the ground is still consecrated),* here turn right. In 150m reach the *Fox and Hounds* ph at Christmas Common. Continue on for a further 250m beyond the public house and at a junction turn left down Hill Rd *(signposted Watlington)*. After 300m turn left into the car park.

Walk 16
Nettlebed, Ewelme Park, Swan's Way, Swyncombe House, Darkwood Farm

Map:	OS Explorer 171
Start/Finish points:	Nettlebed village road side parking
Distance:	13.8kms (8½ miles)
Time:	3½ hrs
Transport Rail:	Nearest is at Henley
Bus:	Nettlebed
Places of interest:	The Kiln, Nettlebed, Pudding stones, Nettlebed, Ewelme Park, St Botolph church Swyncombe
Refreshments:	Nettlebed
Local History Notes:	26, 35
Walk description:	A varied walk of woods, fields, open downland, parkland, hills and views,

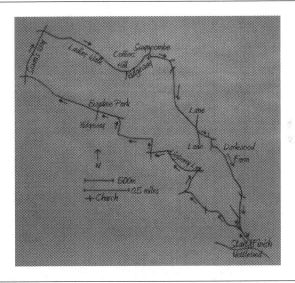

The Route

Leave the junction of Watlington St and the A4130 *(at SU7013 8680)* and walk up Watlington St away from the A4130. Ignore the first footpath on the left and after walking up the road for about 300m, on the left hand side there are two tracks, take the right hand one heading in the same direction amongst tree lines. At a Y-jct bear left and walk behind residences. Continue on this enclosed track which later joins a broad farm track *(at SU6935 8749)*, continue on ahead. Walk through Huntercombe End Farm passing horse stables to join a lane on a bend *(at SU6894 8782)*.

Here turn right and walk along the road, after about 450m and where the lane goes sharp right in front of a residence *(Digberry Farm)*, turn left on a broad track *(Digberry Lane)* on bearing about 280 degrees.

At the end of the broad track and residences go forward past a wide gate and continue on into a wooded area. Continue on the track ahead in the same direction ignoring all others. At a T-jct of tracks *(at SU6861 8854)* turn left. Cross over a broad farm track and continue on the track opposite. In a slight dip in the woodland at a cross track *(at SU6832 8849)* turn right to very soon pass by a wide gate and enter a field. Walk up the left hand side on bearing about 15 degrees. In the top left hand corner of the field turn left through a gap in the tree line and walk along the right hand edge of a field on bearing about 285 degrees. Exit in the right hand corner through a wide gap to enter a smaller field. Continue on the left hand side. Exit the field in the left hand corner following the white arrows and continue on a broad track into woodland. In a further 150m the track turns sharp right. Maintain this track for 300m to reach a surfaced access track *(at SU6774 8911)*, here turn left towards Ewelme Park.

The Kiln, Nettlebed

Pass by cottages and at a Y-jct keep right. At the cross track in Ewelme Park cross over the *Ridgeway Path* and continue ahead down a broad unsurfaced track. Maintain this track and direction for 1.5kms ignoring all other tracks. At a track junction *(at SU6602 8986)* turn right on the *Swan's Way* heading slightly uphill due north. After 800m reach a broad partially surfaced track *(at SU6635 9065)*, here turn right leaving the *Swan's Way*.

In 400m and before the entrance to a private estate, the path bears left round the estate. Exiting from woodland continue to walk round the left hand edge of a field. At the other end of the field follow the track into woodland. At an inverse Y-jct *(at SU6740 9019)* continue on ahead in the same direction. The track gently curves left round Colliers Hill. At a track junction coming on the right *(the Ridgeway at SU6789 8990)* continue on ahead. At a cross track at Swyncombe go forward and round to the right to reach St Botolph church.

St Botolph church, Swyncombe

At St Botolph turn right through the churchyard gate and walk round to the exit at the back, turn left across a green area and then bear right on a track which later crosses the main access drive to Swyncombe House. Continue on alongside a fence line and go through a kissing gate. Continue on ahead on a very faint track in the same direction uphill, *(Swyncombe House is on the right)*. Head for a gate in a tree line on bearing about 100 degrees. Go through the gate *(at SU6864 9010)* and 10m beyond the gate at a Y-jct bear right uphill into woodland. At a track junction cross over the track and continue in the same direction and in a few metres cross over a farm track. Continue on the narrow track opposite and later join a surfaced access drive, here turn left.

At a cottage by a wide gate continue on the track ahead. Later the track becomes a surfaced lane, continue ahead. Eventually the lane reaches the B481 *(at SU6913 8889)*, here turn right.

In 40m cross over the road and turn left on a narrow lane just past a bus shelter. Follow the lane round a sharp right hand bend. Ignore all other paths and at the next right hand bend by a residence *(Wild Wood)* turn left on a track between tree lines. At a junction continue on ahead in the same direction and in 30m *(at SU6950 8859)* bear right on a track *(signed Nettlebed 1 mile)* into a wooded area. Go over a step stile and continue on ahead on a broad grassy track between hedgerows at Darkwood Farm, on the right. Exit over a step stile and go forward past a farm house *(on the left)* and immediately go over another step stile and walk across a field in the same direction. Go over another step stile and continue in the same direction. Aim for the point of a fenced woodland and continue down the left hand side of the field to the very bottom. Go over a step stile and continue in the same direction up a steep field on a faint track on bearing about 150 degrees. The track draws closer to a fenced woodland. At the top of the hill *(at SU6995 8784)* go over a step stile and enter a woodland. The narrow track winds through the woodland for 100m and meets a broad track at a T-jct, here turn left. At a broad cross track *(at SU6996 8773)* turn right uphill. Continue on this track and pass Magpies on the left. Exit to Watlington St and cross over diagonally left and go down Elms Way.

In 20m bear right down a track. In a few metres join the earlier outbound track at a T-jct. Here turn left and re-join Watlington St nearer Nettlebed. Walk down Watlington St to the start/finish point.

Walk 17
Ewelme, Swan's Way, Ridgeway, Ewelme Park, Swyncombe Manor, Swyncombe Downs, Huntingland

Map:	OS Explorer 171
Start/Finish points:	Ewelme cricket field cp, also known as the Common cp or Recreational ground cp at SU6483 9119
Distance:	13.2kms (8¼ miles)
Time:	3¼ hrs
Transport Rail:	None on route
Bus:	Walk can be joined part way round at Nuffield on the A4130 (see below)
Places of interest:	Ewelme village, Ewelme Manor, St Mary the Virgin church Ewelme, Ewelme park, Swyncombe church,
Refreshments:	Shepherds' Hut ph Ewelme (1km off route), Crown ph Nuffield (500m off route), Community shop/cafe Ewelme
Local History Notes:	14, 35
Walk description:	A walk through the history of Ewelme, then taking in views, woods, churches and parks

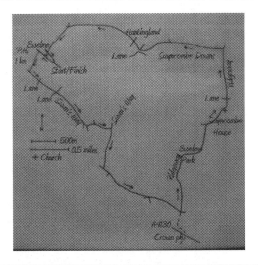

Route

Walk out of the car park at Ewelme cricket field and join the road. Here turn left and take the left fork and pass Ewelme church and C of E primary school on your right.

Continue forward to reach a road on a bend, go forward and in about 100m turn left on a broad track by the Old Coach House *(at SU6450 9142)* and in 60m take a very narrow enclosed track on the right then go over a stile and enter a large field. Continue on up the left-hand edge of the field. In the left-hand corner of the field turn left on a broad enclosed track. In 300m at Day's Lane cross over and continue on the broad track opposite.

Almshouses, Ewelme

Plaque in the almshouses, Ewelme

Cross over an access track and continue on ahead. Exit at a lane and cross over and continue on the surfaced track ahead later joining the *Swan's Way*. When the hard surface ends continue on the track ahead between hedgerows. Maintain this track for 800m emerging at a broad track by farm buildings. Here turn left and in 100m at a Y-junction keep left between hedgerows. Maintain this track and ignore the path on the left, after 400m reach a broad cross track *(at SU6602 8985)*, here turn right leaving the *Swan's Way*.

Walk on the right-hand edge of a field, with a hedge on your right. In about 200m or so where the edge of the field goes left follow the track in the same direction between hedgerows. In 100m ignore the track on the right and continue ahead. The track emerges into a field, continue on ahead on its right-hand edge. Exit in the corner of the field to a broad cross track *(at SU6584 8906)*, here turn left. The track eventually meets the end of an access lane, at residences continue ahead in the same direction. In about 100m at a track junction, on the left, turn left and in 25m turn right on a track between tree lines. At a cross track *(at SU6738 8824)* reach the *Ridgeway*.

(At this junction you may detour to the Crown ph Nuffield or walk back to the bus on the A4130 see below for directions.)

Here, turn left joining the *Ridgeway* and in 20m enter a large field. Walk across the field on a faint track slightly left following the marked tractor lines. Once across the field enter a wooded area. Just after a pond on the right follow the track right. Go through a wide gate and continue on ahead through Ewelme Park. At a cross track in Ewelme Park continue on ahead and in a further 100m just past farm buildings turn right on a broad track. Maintain this track ignoring others. Cross a field and enter a wooded area. The track descends through the wood to a kissing gate, go through the gate and walk across the field exiting through a second kissing gate. Go forward 15m to a broad cross track, here turn right. Continue past the church on the right and at a T-jct turn left. Pass the Old Rectory on the right and walk up to a T-junction of lanes *(at SU6830 9039)*.

Cross over the lane and go through the kissing gate and continue the *Ridgeway* ahead. Follow this track for 1km ignoring others to reach a track junction amongst trees just over the brow of a hill *(at SU6824 9141)*. Here turn left on a track leaving the *Ridgeway*. In a few metres suddenly emerge to a jaw dropping far reaching view. Follow this track which goes alongside an ancient earthwork banking on the left. *(The large house in the mid distance slightly right is Britwell Salome House.)* After 1.1kms at a hard to spot Y-junction *(at SU6724 9156)* bear left and in 10m go through a kissing gate and continue on the grassy track. *(The blot on the landscape dead ahead is Didcot Power Station)*. Go through a second kissing gate and descend into a thickly wooded area. The track finally emerges to a junction of tracks *(at SU6659 9141)* with a nearby lane on the left.

Turn right and in a few metres cross over a broad cross track and continue on the broad track ahead on bearing about 340 degrees, through a field. In 200m at a track junction continue on ahead. Maintain this track which eventually gives way to a narrower track to reach a hard to spot unsigned track junction after 1.5kms *(at SU6512 9197)*, here turn left and enter a field. Walk diagonally half-right on a faint track on bearing about 230 degrees. Once across the field enter a wooded area keeping to the left-hand track. The track emerges to a lane opposite the church in Ewelme.

Here turn left and walk along the lane to a triangular junction of lanes opposite the car park at the cricket ground.

Directions for joining the walk using the bus along the A4130:
From either direction alight at the Crown public house at Nuffield
and join the Ridgeway on the north side of the road. Go through a
kissing gate at SU6749 8786 and continue through woodland on a
winding track. Exit the woodland and walk down and up a field.
Once across the field enter a wooded area and in 15m reach a track
junction. At the cross track you are at SU6738 8824 above. Having
arrived at this point from the south therefore you need to continue
ahead from this point.

Leaving the Ridgeway at this point back returning to the A4130.
From Ewelme turn right and walk across a field on bearing about
200 degrees. Across the field enter a wooded area and follow the
winding path to exit through a kissing gate to join the A4130.

For bus timings please see the useful information and websites at
the back of this book.

Directions to the Crown ph Nuffield are the same directions as for
walking back to the A4130 above.

N.B. At the time of writing the Crown was closed while awaiting a
new tenant.

Directions to the Shepherd's Hut ph:
Turn left out of the start/finish car park and take the left fork (High
St).After 500m at a junction continue on ahead (High St). At a T-jct
turn right along Ayres Lane. The Shepherd's Hut is 200m on the
right.

Directions to the Community shop and cafe, Ewelme:
With your back to the car park walk left along High St passing Days
Lane (on the left) and a pond (on the right), and in a further 20m
turn right into Fibreglass Hill. In 15m cross over to the cafe.

Walk 18
Ewelme, Brightwell Baldwin, Britwell Salome, Ridgeway, Swan's Way

Map:	OS Explorer 171
Start/Finish points:	Ewelme cricket field car park
	at SU6483 9119
Distance:	14kms (8¾ miles)
Time:	3½ hrs
Transport Rail:	None on route
Bus:	None on route
Places of interest:	Ewelme village, Ewelme Manor, St Mary the Virgin church Ewelme, Saint Bartholomew church Brightwell Baldwin, Parish church Britwell Salome.
Refreshments:	Shepherd's Hut ph Ewelme, Lord Nelson ph Brightwell Baldwin, Community shop and cafe, Fibreglass Hill Ewelme.
Local History Notes:	14, 4, 6,
Walk description:	A flatish walk, one hill, taking in villages, churches, green lanes and far reaching views.

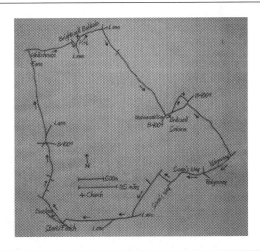

Route

Exit the car park and cross over the triangular junction and walk along Parsons Lane *(signed Britwell Salome)*. Walk on past St Mary the Virgin church to a T-jct.

St Mary the Virgin, Ewelme

Here turn left and in about 100m turn right up Chaucer Court. In

50m turn left and proceed between residences on a stony broad track. At its terminal point after 150m turn right. At the end of the residences go forward on a broad enclosed grassy track. In about 100m go through a wide gate and continue on the track ahead on the left-hand side of a field. In the left hand corner of the field go through a very wide gap in the tree line and continue ahead on the left hand edge of another field. At the top of the field maintain direction on a broad track to the left of a pig farm. Exit the track to join the B4009.

Now you know
what the K stands for!

Cross over the road and continue on the lane opposite. In just over 100m bear left on an enclosed track between tree lines. Maintain this track and direction ignoring all others. After almost 2km reach a broad farm cross track at (SU6422 9481), here turn right and walk across open fields on a broad track on bearing about 90 degrees. Once across the field meet a broad track on a bend, bear left maintaining direction keeping to the left of a tree line. In about 250m where the broad track goes left continue in the same direction and go through a broad gate. Continue on the enclosed track ahead. The track soon emerges to an open field, continue ahead on its right hand edge. Exit in the right hand corner of the field through a wide gate. Continue ahead on an enclosed track. The track exits at a lane, here turn right.

St Bartholomew, Brightwell Baldwin

At the end of the lane meet a road at *(SU6529 9483)*, here turn left and walk along the road into Brightwell Baldwin. Pass by the village church *(Saint Bartholomew)* on the left and the *Lord Nelson* public house on the right, continue on ahead. Having walked through the village turn right on a track opposite Cedar Lodge *(at SU6587 9513 signed Britwell Salome 1.5 miles)*.

Within a few metres go through a wide gate. Continue ahead on a narrower track between hedgerows on bearing about 160 degrees. Exit the track after 2.3kms at a road in Britwell Salome on the B4009 *(at SU6709 9327)*.

At this junction turn left and in less than 200m turn left through a hedgerow and walk on ahead on the right-hand edge of a field. Exit in the right hand corner through a gate and go forward to meet a lane.

Continue on in the same direction along the lane. Walk up to a junction of tracks before the Parish church *(at SU6742 9366)*, here bear right. Go over a cattle grid and through a gate and continue on a track on the left- hand edge of a field. Exit in the left hand corner over a step stile by a wide gate and join a road, the B4009 *(at SU6755 9353)*, here turn right.

In 30m turn left down a broad gravel track *(signed Coopers Farm)*. Maintain direction on this track for 1.5kms ignoring others. At a cross track continue on ahead on a narrower track between hedgerows. Exit the track to meet the *Ridgeway/Swan's Way (at SU6838 9241)*, here turn right on bearing about 230 degrees.

After 400m cross over a lane and continue on ahead.

In a further 350m at a track junction *(at SU6778 9209)* continue on ahead leaving the *Ridgeway* and continuing on the *Swan's Way*. In 800m *(at SU6713 9193)* turn right on a broad track leaving the *Swan's Way* on bearing about 300 degrees. In 300m at a broad cross track turn left. In a further 700m at a cross track *(at SU6648 9160)* cross over it and continue on ahead on a narrower grassy track on the right hand edge of a field. Exit the track at a lane, here turn right.

After 400m along the lane bear right on a track leading up and over a hill. After about 1km and before the end of the field take the left broad grassy track leading downhill towards the cricket field. Exit to a lane opposite the Ewelme cricket field car park.

Directions to the Shepherd's Hut ph:
Turn left out of the start/finish car park and take the left fork (High St).After 500m at a junction continue on ahead (High St). At a T-jct turn right along Ayres Lane. The Shepherd's Hut is 200m on the right.

Directions to the Community shop and cafe:
With your back to the car park walk left along High St passing Days Lane (on the left) and a pond (on the right), and in a further 20m turn right into Fibreglass Hill. In 15m cross over to the cafe.

Local History Notes

1. Assendon

Lower and Middle Assendon were first recorded in 800 A.D. as Assundene which was thought to derive from the Saxon word "denu", meaning a long, narrow, winding valley, and "assa", meaning an ass; together this was translated as the Valley of the Wild Ass. Assundene changed to Afsington and then to Assendene.

The Golden Ball public house at Lower Assendon was, it is said, frequented by the highwaymen Tom King and Dick Turpin.

The Assendon stream has been described as a geographical curiosity which last ran into the river Thames in 2001. Previously it ran in 1969 being the longest absence for the stream running since the 1850's. When the groundwater level in the Stonor house well reaches a critical 85.65 metres the stream rises from the valley floor in a field south of Stonor and begins to flow towards the Thames, it more than often doesn't make it.

2. Bix

The origin of the name Bix is most likely to have been box shrub, a type of evergreen which grows in the parish. The "new" parish church of St James was built in 1875.

A village feature is the Victorian water tank, a brick lined open water tank dating from 1895. It was used for watering horses and for re-filling the local steam engines in addition to supplying the village with water. The tank is situated on the other side of the main road (A4130) just a few metres down the lane opposite and on the right hand side.

On Bix Common Field are ruins of a Roman building. Since excavation it has been re-covered to protect it, nothing can be seen of it today.

3. Bix Bottom

The original Bix church of St James was a small Norman church, which, now in ruins, can still be seen along the road leading to Warburg Nature Reserve and remains on consecrated ground. (It was abandoned in 1875 when the new church was built nearer the main road.) Access was sealed off due to vandalism but it is possible to walk a few metres to it. It has been used as a backdrop in many films. This was the Bix Brand parish church. The font from this church can be seen in the present church of St James.

Archaeologists have discovered an earlier church close by at Bix Bottom which is still being excavated. This was the Bix Gibwyn parish church.

4. Brightwell Baldwin
A bright spring and the name of Sir Baldwin de Bereford once the lord of the manor combine to derive the village name. St Bartholomew's church stands opposite *The Lord Nelson* public house. The church is almost entirely 14th century with earlier suggestions.

Inside there is the oak Parish chest on display which likely dates back to the time that the church was built. St George is depicted on horseback in full armour.

Scenes from the TV series *"Midsomer Murders"* have been filmed in the village.

5. Brightwell Grove (at SU6560 9305 off walks 17 and 18)
Originally a farmhouse built in the 1820's it has been remodelled by David Hicks. Originally a room painted for Lady Mountbatten, at Brook House, London was moved first to Brightwell House then to its present location in Brightwell Grove.

6. Britwell Salome
The parish church of St Nicholas is named after the 4th century Bishop of Myra in Lycia and has stood as the church of Bruttewell Sulham from the 13th century. The earliest church records date from 1234, but more recent dating *(1990's)* of the great yew in the churchyard lends weight to the theory that a church was here long before that. Most of the present church dates from 1867.

To the south west of the village is Britwell Salome House. In its grounds there is a limestone column which was built in 1764 as a monument.

7. Britwell Priory
The priory is an early 17th century house in Britwell Salome.

8. Cadmore End St Mary Le Moor church was designed by Rhodes Hawkins, was consecrated in 1851 and given its present title to commemorate its origins. The original 12th century church at Moor Common was dismantled and rebuilt at Cadmore End. Local farmers were paid to transport the flints and stonework by horse and wagons to its present site.

9. Christmas Common

A small hamlet on the top of Watlington Hill with a few residences and a public house, the *Fox and Hounds*. Nearby there are views overlooking the Oxfordshire countryside. There are various explanations concerning its name, the Christmas family who were local landowners or that there was a truce declared for Christmas Day during the Civil War in 1643.

There was once a church here which is now a private residence, the gravestones are intact. It is still consecrated ground and locals say that burials still take place here.

10. Cookley Green

A small hamlet with a few houses and cottages around the green.

11. Cowleaze Wood

A woodland north of Christmas Common that has a car park.

Within Cowleaze Wood there is an RAF Memorial to the crew of a Halifax bomber LW 579 that crashed here on 31 March 1944. The aircraft was on one of the thousand bomber raids over Germany that night to Nuremburg. Surviving German night fighters and anti-aircraft fire it was just a few miles from the nearest base when it came down in Cowleaze Wood. It was based at RAF Snaith in Yorkshire. All seven members of the crew lost their lives. In all over 100 bombers were lost on that night, the biggest Bomber Command loss of the war. That night's raid was considered a failure due to bombs missing their targets. It is not known why the aircraft crashed. The memorial stone was originally part of Lincoln Cathedral and is inscribed as follows:

> In memory of the crew of 51 Squadron
> Halifax LW579 MH "V"
> Killed in action 31-3-1944
> P/O. Brooks. J.
> F/S. McCormack.D. I.   SGT. Connell. T. S.
> SGT. Kelly. R.   F/S. Churchill. D. A.
> F/S. West. C. W.   F/S. Glass. S.
> To forget is a vain endeavour
> remembrance lasts forever.

12. Ditchfield
A small hamlet near Lane End. The Holy Trinity church is on Ditchfield Common. There is a village pond on the common.

13. Ernie's Gate
Ernie Thomas was a long time Staines Rambler and walks leader who died in 2008 aged 96. He led walks for the Staines Group until he was 93 years of age. He was known to the author.

14. Ewelme
The history of Ewelme in Saxon and earlier days is lost in obscurity. It is said by some that the name itself - Ewelme - is derived from the Latin Aqua Alma, the "sweet water" and by others the name is said to be Anglo-Saxon in origin - from Aewhylme - the "water whelming" up from the ground and so giving rise to those "sweet waters", which spring up on Ewelme Common. Further down the village too are sources in a romantic garden where ageless trout disport themselves in a deep pool, and where children are said to have seen the fairies dancing. From this pool flows, clear and strong, that brook celebrated by Chaucer in these lines:

"In worlde is none more clere of hue, Its water ever freshe and newe, That whelmeth up in waves bright The mountance of three fingers height".

Ewelme is mentioned in the Doomsday Book as La Welme.

Ewelme Manor
Ewelme Manor came into the possession of Thomas Chaucer through his marriage to Matilda Burghersh. He was knighted by Edward III and became Speaker of the House of Commons on five occasions.

In 1540 Henry VIII claimed the Manor as a Royal Residence for himself and is known to have stayed here with Catherine Howard on his honeymoon.

Edward VI granted the Manor of Ewelme to Princess Elizabeth his sister who often visited as a young girl. Later when Queen she visited Ewelme with Robert Dudley, Earl of Leicester who was at the time the Queen's favourite.

There is no record of James I having visited but the Manor was held in trust for Charles I, his sister and her son, but it appears that in 1627 he sold the Manor to Sir Christopher Neville for £4,300.

During the Civil War it was occupied by Prince Rupert.

At the end of the 17th century it was for a time converted into a *'poor man's dwellings'*

The Manor then faded into obscurity until modern times. The lease of the Manor is now in the hands of Ewelme Trustees and the buildings are rented to tenants.

The Almshouses
The Almshouses, St John's Hospital or God's House in Ewelme, were founded in 1437. Today it comprises modernised dwelling for elderly folk.

St Mary the Virgin church
Ewelme church was re-built in 1436 on the site of an older building.

One notable church attendee was the then Prime Minister Mr Asquith while staying at Ewelme Down.

The author Jerome K Jerome author of *Three Men in a Boat* is buried in the churchyard along with his wife, his sister and stepdaughter.

Geoffrey Chaucer (1343-1400), the poet, best known for his *Canterbury Tales,* has connections with Ewelme through his son Thomas.

Inside the church is the Chaucer tomb. Thomas Chaucer (1367-1434) and his wife Matilda Burghersh are commemorated.

Water Cress
The village industry in Ewelme was water-cress cultivated in the bed of Ewelme brook which flows through the village and was sold in Covent Garden market, London. Water-cress is still being cultivated in Ewelme today.

The School
It was founded originally as a Grammar-school, a place of superior education where Latin would be taught by the Grammar-Master. Gradually, however, its prosperity declined, and sometime in the nineteenth century when the attendance had sunk to three or four boys. It was at that time entirely closed and vandalised before later being revived into the state system in the 1830's. It is the oldest school building in the country to be in use as a state primary school.

15. Fawley

The name means *"fallow coloured woodland clearing"*, it was recorded in the Doomsday Book as *Falelie*.

Fawley was the home of Sir Bulstrode Whitelocke who bought the manor of Fawley in 1616. He was a prominent Member of Parliament in Oliver Cromwell's time. There is a Whitelocke monument in the south transept of the church. The Manor House was used by soldiers during the civil war who apparently trashed the place. In 1684 the house was re-designed by Sir Christopher Wren.

St Mary the Virgin church
A church has stood here since the 12th century, the present St Mary the Virgin was re-built in 1748. Later changes took place in Victorian times. Its stained glass window depicts a *Tree of Life* designed by John Piper a local resident and artist. In the grounds of the church are two imposing mausoleums, one built in granite to the Mackenzie family whose ancestor was a successful engineer of Scottish extraction, the other to the Freeman family owners of the Fawley estate. John Freeman being responsible for the re- building of Fawley Court in 1684.

16. Fawley Bottom

John Piper a 20th century artist producing paintings and ceramics and designing stage sets lived at Fawley Bottom farm house *(now a private house)* from 1935 until his death in 1992. He was noted for his wartime paintings of the destruction of Coventry. He designed stained glass windows for Coventry Cathedral. One of his stained glass windows *(Tree of Life)* is in Fawley church.

17. Fawley Hill Railway (Access by invitation only)

This is a private but not secret railway that belongs to a private individual and is operated by a volunteer society.

18. Fingest

Previously Tinghurst or Thinghurst which means "wooded hill where assemblies are made".

The village church is St Bartholomew's and is from the early Norman period and is listed Grade 1.

19. Frieth

The church in Frieth was built in 1848 with later additions. Most of the stained glass windows were a gift from the Cripps family of Parmoor.

20. Hambleden

St Mary's church dates from the 14th century. The Jacobean style manor house was built in 1603. It is said Charles I stayed there overnight while fleeing from Oxford. The Old Rectory was built in 1794. Hambleden was the home of William Henry Smith founder of the bookshop chain WH Smith. He became an MP in 1868 and later was First Lord of the Admiralty, Secretary of State for War, Irish Secretary and First Lord of the Treasury. It is said that the Gilbert and Sullivan song with the line *"now I am ruler of the Queen's Navee"* directly relates to his appointment to the Admiralty. He was the first Viscount Hambleden. His house is past the Stag and Huntsman and beyond the car park. He died in 1891 and is buried in St Mary's churchyard.

Lord Cardigan known for his involvement in the Charge of the Light Brigade was born in the Manor House, *(first left after the church and is on the right.)*

The village has often been used as a film location for such films as *Chitty Chitty Bang Bang, Dance with a Stranger (the true story of Ruth Ellis the last woman to be hanged in Britain for murder) and The Avengers.*

21. Henley and Henley Park

First recorded settlement was in the 12th century. It has many royal connections over the centuries. A world renowned centre for rowing it hosts the annual Henley Royal Regatta.

Henley Park 1½ miles north of Henley on the *Oxfordshire Way* was created in the 13th century as a medieval deer park of Fawley Court. The house was previously a Dower house of Fawley Court.

22. Ibstone

The origins of Ibstone can be traced back to the 8th century, the name derives from Ibba's Stones. Its Doomsday record is Hibestanes.

North of the cricket field is a standing stone.

The 900 year old church of St Nicholas is separate from the village.

Barbara Castle the former Member of Parliament and Minister lived in Ibstone in a house named Hell Corner Farm.

23. Luxters Farm Micro Brewery and Vineyard

Situated on Dudley Lane off Skirmett Lane, Luxters brew their own ales and produce their own wines. They have a cellar shop. Car park opposite.

24. Maidensgrove

A very small hamlet west of Stonor. Maiden's Grove Farm now a private residence dates from the 17th century.

25. Moor Common

Here once stood the 12th century Ackhampsted Chapel which was dismantled and rebuilt at Cadmore End (St Mary Le Moor).

26. Nettlebed

The origin of the village is unknown but may have been named after the nettles which grow in abundance in the area. Sheets and table cloths were made from nettles in the 18th century.

For the last 1000 years there has been a church in Nettlebed. The present St Bartholomews was completed in 1846 and incorporates parts of the original Norman tower. It has stained glass windows by local artist John Piper of Fawley.

Nettlebed has a remaining kiln. Bricks were produced originally by the Flemings (Flemish) in Nettlebed and continued until the 1930's. Local bricks and tiles can be seen in buildings in the High St, Ewelme school and Stonor House.

The large house called Joyce Grove was bought by Robert Fleming in 1903. Descendents of Robert Fleming are Peter Fleming the traveller and writer who was married to Celia Johnson, the actress, *(Brief Encounter)*, also Ian Fleming the author of the James Bond books. Both Peter and Celia are buried in the local churchyard.

To the north east of Nettlebed is Windmill Hill where indeed there was once a windmill. The last one burned down in 1912. It was situated about 500m up Mill Lane.

Two pudding stones are displayed at a road junction by a bus shelter. The pudding stones were used by the ancient Britons as signposts standing in a line from Grimes Ditch in Norfolk to the Thames at Pangbourne, they are about 4000 years old.

27. Northend
A small village with a duck pond.

28. Parmoor
St Katherine's in the parish of Parmoor has changed its usage since the fourteenth century when it was owned by the Knights Templar. It was once a Convent and is now an ecumenical retreat and conference centre.

It was once the family home of the Cripps family. Sir Stafford Cripps was born here and became the Chancellor of the Exchequer.

During WWII it was the refuge of King Zog of Albania and his family from 1941 to 1946. They were helped to England from France by Ian Fleming, author of the James Bond books who was then a naval officer.

29. Pishill
The name of Pishill, meaning 'the hill on which peas grow'.

The 12th century parish church of St Paul's has a stained glass window designed by John Piper of Fawley Bottom. The north aisle of this church is unusual in that from the pews it is possible to see the pulpit but not the altar. Referred to as the Stonor aisle it may have allowed the Roman Catholics from Stonor to use the church after it became protestant.

30. Red Kites
These distinctive birds of prey were re-introduced to the Chilterns from Spain between 1989-1994 as they had become extinct in England by the end of the 19th century through egg collecting, poisoning and shooting. A penny was offered for each bird dead or alive.

A red kite has a wingspan of between 1.5 – 1.7m (5ft – 5.5ft) and weighs between 900 – 1300g (2 – 3lbs). They feed on carrion, sometimes small mammals and worms and beetles. They begin to breed in their second or third year and lay their eggs (1 - 4) usually in April. They incubate for about 30 – 34 days. The young stay in their nests for about seven to eight weeks before attempting to fly. They often live for twelve or more years.

31. Russell's Water.
A small village of Chiltern charm. It has a delightful village pond where some scenes of the film *Chitty Chitty Bang Bang* were filmed.

32. Skirmett
A settlement 2 miles north of Hambleden. Of Norse origin its name means *"Shire meeting place"*.

It once had a church, a mid 19th century flint construction which is now a private house and is situated just past *The Frog* towards Turville.

It has a village hostelry called *The Frog*. Oh yes, *"Skirmett the Frog"*, it's true I tell you, the pub was re-named from the King's Head.

The village policeman was housed in Hope Cottage, now a private residence.

At the end of the village is a house with a crooked chimney – can you spot it?

33. Southend
A village in the middle of nowhere on the road to somewhere.

34. Stonor
Stonor has been the home of the Camoy family for over 800 years. The house is built on the site of a prehistoric circle. Its medieval Catholic chapel was in continuous use during Catholic repression. It afforded a sanctuary for St Edmund Campion in 1581.

The Stream – now you see it, now you don't
A geographical curiosity in that it rarely reaches its outlet at the River Thames. It last ran to the Thames in 2001 and before that in 1969 making it the longest absence for 150 years. On average every 40 years it causes flooding due to its sudden fast flowing. When the ground water level reaches a critical depth of 85.65 metres in the Stonor House well the water rises from a field south of Stonor and begins to flow. When the water level falls the stream stops.

35. Swyncombe
The name Swyncombe means "valley where pigs are kept".

The church of St Botolph is 1,000 years old. Swyncombe House with its cluster of farm buildings is nearby. This settlement dates from Saxon times. The small Norman church was probably constructed in the 11th century of flint and stone. There has been a manor house here for hundreds of years, although the present manor house at Swyncombe is a 19th century re-build of an Elizabethan house.

36. The Chiltern Hills
The Chiltern Hills were declared an Area of Outstanding Natural Beauty (AONB) in 1965. They are a range of chalk hills stretching 75 miles from South West to North East, from Goring to Hitchin.

37. The Chiltern Hundreds
By established custom Members of Parliament (MP's) may apply for stewardship of the Chiltern Hundreds as a device to resign their seats.

38. Turville
The name derives from Anglo-Saxon for *"dry field"*. There has been a church here since the 12th century. The present church, St Mary the Virgin, had additions of a north aisle built in 1733 to accommodate a grander pew for the then Lord of the Manor, William Perry, the great grandfather of the poet Percy Bysshe Shelley. The stained glass window was designed by John Piper of Fawley Bottom.

The village of Turville is the location site for the TV series *"The Vicar of Dibley"*. The windmill seen on the hill to the north east of the village is Cobstone Windmill which was a film location in the film *"Chitty Chitty Bang Bang"* as the workshop of *"Caracatus Potts"*.

Turville was the home of Sir John Mortimer, lawyer and dramatist, he lived at Turville Heath Cottage.

Notice the old school sign at the lane junction on the left before the church gate.

39. Turville Court
A private residence.

40. Turville Grange

A mid 18th century house was once occupied by Princess Lee Radziwill the US socialite and sister of Jackie Kennedy. She shared the house with her second husband who was a Polish prince.

41. Turville Park

A late 17th century house. A grade II listed building and the home of Lord Sainsbury the supermarket owner.

42. White Mark

A chalk carving on the hillside above Watlington. It is 270 feet high and 36 feet wide. It is said to have been designed in 1764 by the local squire Edward Horne so that the Norman church of St Leonard in Watlington looked to have a spire when viewed from his house.

43. Wormsley Park

A 2500 acre estate with an 18th century country house where Sir Paul Getty II once lived. He lived there from 1986 until his death in 2003. The cricket field is a replica of the Oval built after Mick Jagger introduced him to cricket. John Major then the Prime minister and the Queen Mother attended the first match played there in 1992 along with Michael Caine, Dennis Compton, and Brian Johnston. Others who have played the game there are Andrew Flintoff, Imran Khan, Peter O'Toole, Mike Gatting, Derek Randall, Tim Rice, Michael Atherton, Mark Ramprakash, Mike Brearley and Rory Bremner. Teams that have played on the ground include the Australians, West Indians, Sri Lankans and South Africans.

44. Warburg Nature Reserve

A reserve of 248 acres of woodland, grassland in a dry valley. It is open to the public every day except Bank Holidays and has its own car park *(not to be used for walkers or cyclists)*. There is an information centre there.

The record of Chiltern history from the earliest times is beyond the scope of this book.

Useful addresses and websites

Rambler's Association, 2nd Floor, Camelford House, 89 Albert Embankment, London SE1 7TW, Tel: 020 7339 8500 Fax: 020 7339 8501 www.ramblers.org.uk Email: ramblers@london.ramblers.org.uk

Ordnance Survey www.ordnancesurvey.co.uk Tel: 08456 050505 or 023 8079 2000

National Trust www.nationaltrust.org.uk Tel: 0870 609 5380

Countryside agency www.countryside.gov.uk Tel: 020 7340 2900

English Heritage www.english-heritage.org.uk Tel: 0870 333 1181

English Nature www.english-nature.org.uk Tel: 01733 455100

Chiltern Society www.chilternsociety.co.uk

Find an address www.mapquest.co.uk

Guide to taxis serving all railway stations www.traintaxi.co.uk

Details of taxis www.cabnumbers.com

Met office www.metoffice.gov.uk Tel: 0870 900 0100 or 01392 885680

Buckinghamshire County Council
www.buckscc.gov.uk

Oxfordshire County Council
www.oxfordshire.gov.uk

Tourist Information Centres
www.tourist-information.com

Travel Information

Buses
www.travelinesoutheast.org.uk Tel 0871 200 2233

www.arrivabus.co.uk

www.thames-travel.co.uk

Rail
www.nationalrail.co.uk

Chiltern Railways
www.chilternrailways.co.uk

Index